CW01310239

THE MONEY CODE

Free, Wise and Rich

RAIMON SAMSÓ

EDICIONES

The editors have not verified the efficacy or the result of the recipes, products, technical formulas, exercises or similar contained in this book. They urge readers to consult a doctor or health specialist in case of any doubt that may arise. They do not assume, therefore, any responsibility

Regarding their use, they do not provide advice in this regard.

Copyright by Raimon Samsó / Instituto Expertos S.L.

1st edition: January 2019

Cover design: D. Sharma

© 2019, Raimon Samsó

© 2019, Instituto Expertos, S. L. (All rights reserved for this edition)

Edit: Ediciones Instituto Expertos

Principe de Vergara 109 2nd

28002 Madrid

Spain

All rights reserved. No part of this publication, including the cover design, may be reproduced, stored, transmitted or used in any way by any means, electronic, chemical, mechanical, optical, recording or electrographic, without prior written consent of the editor.

Ask always permission at: info@raimonsamso.com

Contents

Introduction ix

Part I
Financial Freedom

1. Winning Financial Freedom 3
2. Regain Your passion and Your Life 9
3. How to Overcome Crisis 15
4. Why are there Economic Problems? 21
5. The 4 Obstacles to Financial Freedom 31
6. Retirement, the Financial Future that is Uncertain 35
7. Do you Live in a World that No Longer Exists? 41
8. Globalization is Here to Stay 47
9. Financial Intelligence and Financial Freedom 53
10. What They Didn't Tell You About Money 61
11. Applied Financial Intelligence 67
12. Awareness and Money 73
13. The Vocabulary of Wealth 79
14. 30 Questions to Make You Think 83
15. The Change has Already Begun 87
16. The 4 Cardinal Rules of Work 97
17. The 3 Roles and the Corresponding Income 101
18. Working for Yourself 107
19. The 9th Wonder of the World - the Notion of Passive Income 111
20. Leverage: the Force that Moves Mountains 119
21. Invest or Gamble? 125
22. Optimal Debt and Bad Debt 133
23. The Money Code 139

Part II
From Employee to Entrepreneur

24. Common Excuses for Not Taking the First Step 145
25. The 3 Secrets to Successful Undertakings 153

26. Deliver significant value to massive numbers of people	157
27. Secret of Money: to Serve	161
28. Turn your talent into income.	165
29. The 12 Indispensable Skills Entrepreneurs	169
30. Please don't be "self-employed entrepreneur."	175
31. The Happy Business Curve	179
32. Start Small, Think Big	183
33. Starting on the Right Foot	187
34. Act and you'll be lucky.	191
35. The Keys to Undertaking and Starting	197
36. Your Business Needs a Super and Irresistible Product	203
37. Use a Proven Success Model	207
38. System, System, System!	211
39. Profitable Management of Your Time	215
40. Common "Shipwrecks"	221
41. Learn to Sell (if you're going to be in business)	227
42. Catchy Ads that Sell	233
43. Multi-level Marketing Option	237
44. "I", registered trademark	241
45. Promote Yourself	245
46. Building a Website that Sells	249
47. Your Online Service Providers	253
48. Your Irresistible Internet Marketing	255
Afterword	261
About the Author	265
Note	273

To my parents.

If I think of my parents in terms of the lottery, I certainly hit the jackpot: they gave me love, knowledge and freedom.

Probably because that's what they stood for.

My greatest desire is that all parents in the world, me included, will someday hear the same words from their own children.

Introduction

In my profession as a coach, I know that to achieve something different, a person must first be different and must do different things. An aspect of our life will improve when we improve ourselves, but not before then. Always in that order.

Money is no exception to this rule. So for our economy to change, we have to "change" ourselves. This book discusses that personal change and on doing different things.

In my everyday work with people, I have realised that people very often want their circumstances to improve without first improving their way of thinking. The rule of law and order teaches us that "we are our beliefs." We cannot force external circumstances and change them into what they are not. The question that anyone should ask, sooner or later is: Do my beliefs agree with my desires?

It is paradoxical, but the people who most need to change are precisely the ones who are most reluctant to change, the most inflexible. Perhaps they think that to change their opinions is a sign of weakness. At the same time, they feel uncomfortable when they are told that their own inflexibility is what distances them from their desires.

Introduction

This book recommends changes in our beliefs about money. Without an open mind, all of the answers will slip through the cracks. The Money Code holds information that is meaningful from a certain mindset - the kind of mindset which this book wishes to develop in readers who are ready and willing to embrace it.

The money code provides answers to questions we've all asked ourselves about financial freedom, and yet I already know that not all of the answers here will be welcome.

As a matter of fact, I don't believe that problems exist; what exist are solutions that we do not like. Our problems, of course, are not in the world but in our mental perceptions, contemplating upon them. Solutions to money problems require unlearning all that has proven to be ineffective. This book proposes a paradigm change in stereotype thinking about money.

It is said that every life is a reflection of one's decisions, habits, choices, beliefs, emotions and behaviours that lead right up to the present condition of a person's life. And for as long as someone believes that his money problems have nothing to do with his mentality and behaviour, that person will continue to have from money problems.

I have learned that economic problems are not caused by money itself, but by thought patterns about it. In normal circumstances, personal finance is a reflection of a person's thinking, his behaviour and the decisions he makes.

My conclusion: in reality, money resides in the mind.

Almost everything that the average person knows about money is based on opinions that have been conditioned and which have accumulated throughout his life. Economic success is a type of mental programming (think of numbers with many zeros) and that economic failure - the opposite - is yet another type of programming (this time think of numbers with only a few zeros). In both cases, it comes down to a piece of software or programming device installed in the brain: in the money game, this software

Introduction

becomes a losing or winning programme. This book will help people to re-programme themselves so they can achieve prosperity.

The difference between people who are prosperous and those who are not lies in the first group's application of useful formulas; in the second group, it is their application of useless or ineffective formulas.

This book will teach you how to distinguish one from the other. I suggest that you study it well and bring it with you everywhere - the way you take a good friend to your favourite place - until you have mastered the contents. It is meant to be read, re-read, underlined, and annotated. My wish is that you make this book a reference book for when you decide to become an entrepreneur with your own personal business. And I'd like you to consider me as your financial coach. I can help you improve your relationship with money.

What follows is a list of the biggest and most glaring lies I heard about money. They are unfounded myths, superstitions and prejudices. I have found that there are more problems with the idea of "what someone knows but is not sure" than with "what someone does not know".

What follows are some (not all) irrational beliefs about money: *"money does not interest me", "you cannot be rich and be spiritual at the same time", "you have to work hard to become rich", "I may be poor but at least I'm honest", "to be poor is more noble and spiritual", "the rich are bad people", "you can't have fun and earn money", "I'm not good with money", "if I win, someone else loses", "there isn't enough money for everyone", "it is worth knowing more about the bad than knowing about the good", "money is not important", "money corrupts", "the more money you make, the more taxes you pay", "money can't buy happiness", "money is dirty"...*

Just mentioning and writing these down exhausts me. Do you now understand why there are so many economic problems?

If you admit believing in any of the statements I mentioned, don't let that bother you. Don't feel guilty. The fact is, what you believed

Introduction

before and today are not important; what is important is what you choose to believe in from now on, going forward.

Let's be clear about this: I don't think it is a contradiction that things are going well with you and that you're doing a great service to others.

People generally do not make a connection between their beliefs and money because to them, these two seem unrelated. This book explains why there is a relationship. The years I spent working in a bank have taught me that the concept of prosperity constitutes a kind of "mental baggage". And my years as an entrepreneur have taught me all the lessons you're about to learn.

Every person who learn the ideas in this book - ideas I develop in my courses - have in some way, changed their economic life. My desire is to contribute to the financial education of people to alleviate their suffering caused by economic reasons.

This book is also about the changes the world is experiencing and the need to have a new way of thinking, because I know that when the rules of the game are changed, there is a need to adjust the way the game is played. Do you know the rules of the new economy? Let me tell you what I know about this subject.

Right now, there are millions of people around the world who earn a salary but do not have a life; they're pining for financial freedom, aching to quit their jobs and create a new and more meaningful lifestyle for themselves. I believe - and I will also point out that this is an accurate statement today - that people need a jolt, a shock treatment, to wake up from the dream that keeps so many of them chained to a job that they don't love, and therefore preventing them from acquiring wealth and freedom.

However, I do not wish to offend anyone nor impose my views on them. Please - all I ask is that you consider what you're about to read as a personal matter. For my part, I promise to write about money without the fluff and filler.

Introduction

When I refer to the educational system, please don't feel that I am alluding to you personally if you happen to be a teaching professional. For me, teachers at all levels are heroes and heroines who do so much for so little. My sister is a teacher who works with teens, and I know firsthand that her day-to-day is more difficult than any of us can imagine. I confirm my appreciation of, and respect for, all teaching professionals.

This book has two parts: "Financial Freedom" - the money code - and "From Employee to Entrepreneur" - the money code in Action. The first part focuses on attitudes, the second on aptitude which constitute the heads and tails of the same coin: economic success. While writing this book, I try to explain financial concepts using simple, everyday language that everyone can understand, and I hope I have achieved this.

In the first part we shall examine the following: what is happening, why there are economic problems, what are the obstacles to financial freedom, and what is financial intelligence and financial freedom. I'll reveal what is not taught in school and what keeps people trapped in the race for survival. You will learn about the three roles people choose to play to create income. You will also learn the vocabulary of wealth.

There's more.

You will discover the ninth wonder of the world - the notion of passive income. And finally, you will unlock the money code.

In the second part, you will learn: how an entrepreneur thinks and behaves, how to avoid common mistakes, how not to stagnate in a job, the importance of having a super product and a perfect system that works alone, how to start an irresistible marketing campaign and with what means, how to develop entrepreneurial skills, how to do more with less (thanks to ? how to promote yourself with ?, how to choose the ideal clients, how to position your personal brand, and how to tap the power of the Internet to develop your personal business.

Introduction

The money code contains information that blow off those thought patterns that prevent people from becoming free and prosperous. I know what those thought patterns are, and I'd like to warn you about them. I won't tell you what to do, when to do it, or how to do it; neither will I tell you what kinds of business work and which ones don't.

The aim of this book is to unleash the financial IQ of all those reading this book. What each one does afterwards is their choice and their responsibility.

This book is for people who are employed, but who are dissatisfied with their work; it is also for those who already have their own personal business, but feel they must take it to the next level. I wrote it for people who are prepared to improve their financial situation. In effect, this is a book for everyone because we all handle money every day.

Raimon Samsó, bestselling author

PART I

Financial Freedom

1

Winning Financial Freedom

THIS IS the easiest part of the book because it does not deal with learning but with "unlearning." Whatever you want to achieve becomes possible after the process of subtraction, not addition. Do not seek financial freedom, it is better to get rid of all the barriers that come between you and this financial freedom. Eliminate the obstacles and nothing will separate you from what you seek. This book is intended to help you unlearn what you thought you knew about money, and what simply isn't true.

I'm going to make a confession: My present income does not come from the traditional education I had. Nor is my present financial freedom the fruit of my university studies. The years I spent studying Macroeconomics, Financial Mathematics, Statistics, Econometrics, Economic History or Commercial Law did not make me earn a Euro all my life. Pity.

I confess that what I learned about money and other matters worth knowing were not taught to me at the university where I graduated with a degree in Economic Sciences, nor did I learn them from the three multinational companies where I was in charge of Finance;

and I certainly didn't learn them from the three banks where I worked. In fact, I learned the money code from my own system by creating multiple incomes, and in these pages I will happily share them with you.

Yes, during my transition from employee to entrepreneur, I learned some key lessons. And this book is the quintessence of the most interesting period of my life. More and more people ask me how they can transition from being an employee to an entrepreneur. I always suggest a process of coaching which will support them and ensure a smooth, well-planned transition; nothing traumatic at all.

Starting an independent professional activity is not a simple process - it is the force of inertia, in addition to overcoming the fears, mustering up a lot of courage and commitment, as well as a limitless amount of discipline and patience. I also suggest to start small. Invest a small amount of money but a lot of talent and creativity, because I know that initially, mistakes will be made.

Infinite patience and discipline are the attitudes that generate the most profit.

The key, as always and in everything, is to love and enjoy the process. If targets are important, the process of achieving them is even more important. The great gift of life is who you become as you pursue and achieve your goals.

The same goes for money; you get more if you don't focus on making money per se, but instead focus on the enjoyment of serving people. If you do it this way, you can be sure that the money will come.

The secret to getting money is not chasing after it.

There are two groups of people when it comes to money:

1. People who *need* to earn money immediately (they work for money).
2. People who *choose* to increase their income in the medium term (they work for assets).

When you don't have a pressing need for money, it is much easier to create wealth. When you need it immediately, you reduce your chances of making money; all that's left for you is to work for money. So I often say that economic prosperity is not achieved in a job, but outside the job.

Prosperity is an effect, and its cause are the beliefs one holds about money and financial education. Everyone who learns how to activate the causes of prosperity inevitably acquire material wealth. *"Inside each life lie the causes of what goes into it,"* said F.W. Sears, author of *How to Attract Success*.

Admittedly, money loves that who loves the process, and not the one who loves the result. The first is the cause and the second is the effect. A strategy focused on the effects is as absurd as expecting to win the lottery without buying a ticket.

Money is the inevitable effect of activating its causes. Do you know them?

We must be taught, from a young age, that this is not a world of things but of "ideas that have solidified." That reality is an emanation of the mind. And everything that happens in the material world was created before the individual or collective mind. "If you see it in your mind, you will see it in reality", but if you cannot create it in your mind, it won't go anywhere. Yes, "thoughts are things" - repeat that with me so you do not forget it. Money is also an idea, a concept, so you must create it before it is created in the mind. Since you have the ability to create thoughts, you can create wealth.

Is money an idea? Yes, money is an idea!

It seems like a clever play of words, but it isn't. It's a solid concept, you can almost touch it because it is real. Money is an "amplifier" of your beliefs, it expands what is already in you. If your programming comes from a poor mentality, money will be tight; if your programming comes from a wealthy mindset, money will be aplenty. Money reveals the idea you have about it, no more, no less.

Allow me to state a metaphor: people incorporate a "mental thermostat" that marks the maximum limit on the money they allow themselves to have. What is the "economic temperature" that marks your thermostat? It's easy to find it: examine your tax return, your bank statements, your income figures... Do not make excuses about it, these constitute the "thermometer" that defines your inner limits.

Poor thoughts, poor behaviour, poor results. Rich thoughts, rich behaviour, rich results.

Some people say: "Money is not important." I agree, but at the same time, I don't. I have arguments for those who say it is and for those who say it is not.

For those who say that money is not important:

In general, people who make this statement live in fairness; they state it with a sigh. Their beliefs are reflected in their economic life and they do not have sufficient money because for them, "it is not important". I wonder, how can they achieve something of no value? Because when they state that something is "not important", what they're doing is getting away from themselves.

I have some questions for those who say that money is "not important": if it's not important, why spend 40 hours or more a week in a job for 40 years or more? And why do they accept to be on the payroll at the end of the month? If it is not important, then it is not necessary ...or is it?

See how it is important?

Two additional questions for those who are not yet clear about it.

One: if they had a hundred million Euros tomorrow, would they be doing the same thing in the same manner, and for the same number of hours each day?

Two: If they had five years left to live, would they be doing the same thing?

And for those who say that money is important:

Generally, I don't want to spend life working just to earn money. Since they don't want to always worry about money, they solve this issue once and for all so they can enjoy life. They learn the rules of the money game and apply them. They get in shape financially. They do their homework and don't wait until the last minute to prepare for the exam. As an issue that is important to them, they solve it right away and then focus on living.

Sir Richard Branson, founder of the Virgin empire, said that all people come to him ask about his secret for making money. But what he actually sees is that what people want to know is how they can make money because, he says, everyone wants to be a millionaire. The answer he gives them is: "I try to have fun. What good is spending all their time working until they're exhausted? Having fun refreshes you and stimulates you at a spiritual level. Knowing how to laugh at yourself, to love, and appreciate others is what life is all about." Thank you, Mr. Branson for clarifying this.

Make no mistake, money is not important to what isn't, and is important to what it is.

We agree that money influences many areas of our lives. For example, the lack of money is one of the leading causes of anxiety, many couples break up because of discussions about money problems, and too many lives are not lived fully because of a lack of money. Statistics tell us that financial problems are the leading cause of divorce (it's not a lack of love but the lack of money). These financial problems may even mean the difference between life or death in some situations.

What follows is something I did not write myself; it's from the pen of Dostoyevsky: *"Money is coined liberty."* I totally agree. Money buys the freedom for us to choose what to do with our time.

I know very well that money cannot buy happiness, but I know too that the lack of money cannot make you happy. It's been proven. Okay, money does not buy happiness, but you are so close to it that you can start your "happiness walk" in just a few minutes. In fact, money creates a mental state that is so close to happiness that even a skilled neurologist can tell the difference. Kidding aside, when you're not feeling pressured about the need to make money, you stop worrying every minute about where the next euro or dollar will come from, and you can start feeling rich and free!

2

Regain Your passion and Your Life

PEOPLE WHO TAKE MY "FINANCIAL FREEDOM" course are seeking to take control of their financial destiny. They are men and women who want to take responsibility for their economic situation and become financially independent. They are people who are tired of going through the same things and not getting anywhere. If you are reading this book, I bet you're one of those people. Like them, you probably feel that the time has come to take charge of your financial destiny.

Let's get started then.

My opinion about keeping a job as the sole source of income is quite radical and I do not expect everyone to agree with this opinion. My personal point of view is that it is foolhardy to rely on only one source of revenue. To depend on employment is a risk we should protect ourselves from.

Let's face it, a "regular job" is not safe, it is but an illusion of security. If anyone expects to achieve "job security", that person has lost all sense of reality. The "secure job" mentality is similar to the situation of dinosaurs: it's about to be extinct. See if you can eliminate the concept of "employment insurance" from your vocabulary.

Whoever misses this concept can always look for it in the museums of history.

Believe me, there is no such thing as security. Security is a fantasy. *"Security is only a superstition, there is no such thing in the natural state of things. Life is an adventure or it is nothing"*. These were the words of Helen Keller (she was born deaf and blind, but she learned to speak, graduated from college, wrote books, and gave lectures on self-improvement throughout her life. As a result of her works, she received recognition from the American government). Someone finally spoke clearly on this subject.

No boat is safe once it leaves the harbour, but ships are built to sail the seas, not to venture out in search for safety. My opinion is that in the future, the only security we can have is: a) maintaining one's creativity in life and b) re-learning how to live. If we are capable of creating usefulness and meaning, adding value to our life constantly, then and only then will we not lack in income.

Some people work their entire lifetime at a job to survive, others work to create an asset or set up a business from which they can live on for the rest of their lives. Do you see the difference? I do.

Look, if you work in a job, you have to work harder each time to earn the same salary. If you create an asset, on the other hand, you work less until you start working for yourself. An asset can earn ten times more than a salary and you work ten times less. Can you see the huge difference between the two? This paragraph summarizes some of what I did **not** hear from my teachers in school. When I think of it, I cannot believe it.

Yes, you understood correctly. Rich minds create assets that generate cash flow, while poor minds create more liabilities that absorb more and more money. I believe that everyone should learn the difference between assets and liabilities:

$$\text{Assets} = \text{create money}$$
$$\text{Liabilities} = \text{cost money}$$

The difference between assets and liabilities is your net worth. Could you stop reading for a moment and calculate your approximate net worth? In the meantime, I'll make myself a cup of tea...

I'm back. If the difference is positive but it isn't enough, continue reading. If the number is negative, you're bankrupt. Continue reading. To all readers: become experts in creating assets, not specialists in creating liabilities.

There are more differences. When you get a job, you have to work, when you get an asset, it starts working for you. While most people spend their lives studying in order to work and thus receive a pay check, others spend their time creating assets to ensure their retirement.

At this time, it is now easier to work creating assets for yourself and this never been possible before in history.

Why is an asset better than a job? Because you cannot own a job; you can own an asset. Because you cannot sell a job but yes, you can sell an asset. Because a job does not pay you money when you stop working; an asset, however, will continue to give you money after you have stopped working. Is this clear? (reader, mark this paragraph!).

Again, I think that to depend economically on a job was part of a model that worked well in the past but these days, it offers only doubts. I understand that a person who values a job and a pay check above all, or to a person who knows of no other way of earning income, may find this statement shocking. But in the next 15 years, the labour force, as we know it in the West, will probably be unrecognizable. In the post-industrial economy, the notion of work will change in more ways than it has in the previous two centuries.

Today, the world is changing at an unprecedented rate.

Everything is changing so rapidly that in Europe, politicians, labour unions, and workers are unable to understand it. What they say do not correspond to the changes that lie ahead. We are at present transitioning to a service economy where the raw materials are talent, innovation, technology and knowledge. The jobs that will remain will be mostly in the so-called McJobs (in dubious honour of McDonalds), characterized by high staff turnover and low pay. With such expectations, who still wants a job?

Looking for a job has the obvious consequence of having a *lot of work*. Worse, it will be a case of being buried under a mountain of work. The next thing that happens is this: a worker becomes so busy at work that he does not have the time to think about how to get rich.

Speaking of rich...

Amancio Ortega, Mr. Zara, is a self-made man. He created the Inditex Group, Zara's flagship company; it has branches all over the world. He is the tenth richest man in the world and the richest in Spain. The key to all this success was the innovative system of his clothing chains. Regarding his two innovation projects, he says: "The Ponte dos Brozo project and the Technology and Development Centre share the same goal - that of promoting innovation. The first lies in the education field and the second is in helping to demonstrate that human development and technological revolution are a source of prosperity." His key: innovation.

The future of Europe, the USA, and Japan is in innovation, not in production. Innovation: everything that smells fresh. Remember that.

Today we are witnessing a perplexing transition from full employment to full unemployment; this latter situation does not mean a chaotic labour market, but a different labour market requiring flexibility, facing changes on the job, accepting low hourly pay, and getting into low-quality contracts. This is happening and, without getting into assessments, it might be better to ask ourselves: How can we prepare ourselves to overcome the disadvantages of this scenario?

The change lies in the world and will remain there (as background noise). The good news is that the changes bring about opportunities commensurate to the speed of change (which is frenetic). In fact, every time there is a change (whether they are technological, market, or requirement changes...) great opportunities emerge. And what about you? Are you waiting for your opportunity, looking for it, or creating it?

I think Europeans are being jolted by the phenomenon of globalization but they don't have the ability to anticipate, respond, and adequately react to this change. The Anglo-Saxons, both Europeans and Americans, are more flexible to change. What we know is that the greatest opportunities come to those who move quickly within the context of change. Those who are slow lose their options and pay a high price for this rigidity. Flexible thinking wins, rigid thinking loses. Those who do not see opportunities in change will suffer.

Any job, however good, cannot bring you true freedom or make you rich. The term "workstation" is a paradigm that fails in all respects, like oil leaking from a car. I'm not saying that no one enjoys being in a job (it's true that some people do enjoy their jobs but they are the exception); relying on a job to live, however, can be expensive from a financial point of view.

I hope we now agree that the passport to freedom and prosperity is: "my own personal business." Sounds good, yes?

- *Your time is yours*, who else owns it but you? And where is it written that your time must be used in something with which you're not convinced?
- *Your finances are yours*, who else owns it but you? And what sense does it make to follow financial recommendations that do not work?
- Your freedom is yours, who else owns it but you? Isn't freedom the most fundamental right of a human being?

Yes, your life belongs to you. And the next thing I say to you - you have to conquer it. Agreed, it's yours, but you must earn it. Let's be sincere about it, what belongs to you does not mean it's free.

3

How to Overcome Crisis

WHEN SPEAKING OF CRISIS, we focus more on the problem than the solutions. The downside is that we don't usually like these solutions. The most effective solutions are those that we like less (this is a proven fact). The final solutions are often the ones that make us most uncomfortable because they call into question our old beliefs and habits... It is no coincidence that the most unpleasant solutions are truly the most effective.

In addition to the crisis, another structural phenomenon is happening in the background and is here to stay: globalization. They are the two different phenomena that today overlap in time. Crisis is temporary (conjectural), globalization is structural. One will go, the other stays. When the crisis ends, we realise that we face a much more complex economic climate: the global economy.

Things will never be as they were before.

One effect of globalization is off-shoring; it is starting now with the "blue-collar jobs" and will extend to the "white-collar jobs" eventually. The manager who prepares the employment adjustment file does not realise that he may be the next in line.

Sitting around and hoping that the crisis will pass (or ignoring globalization) is the worst approach. Let's compare this situation to eating: after we finish the first course (crisis), we are then served the second meal (globalization). I doubt very much that the average person is prepared for this second course.

For example, a person is unemployed and repeats to himself that "nothing comes out of this for me." Perhaps "what is his" is no longer necessary or no longer worth having. So why don't we recycle it, perhaps he needs to open a suitcase of memories to find "his thing."

The average person thinks that the crisis is the problem that needs to be solved, but he is not aware that his poor financial education exacerbated his situation even before the crisis occurred and left him defenceless in the face of globalization.

Crises are natural processes, they are part of the expansion and contraction of life, like a heartbeat. They'll always be there. When the media are obsessed about creating a bad atmosphere, this provides an additional excuse for those people to use them to throw in the towel. A crisis can be an excuse for not taking action.

How do we prepare for economic development in both phenomena: the presence of crisis and globalization? I think I have the answers:

If your job turns you into a computer, find another job.

If your job turns you into a robot, look for another job.

If your job is based on experience, look for another job.

If your job is not creative, look for another job.

If your job does not bring meaning to your life, look for another job.

If your job is too manual, find another job.

If your job can be digitised, find another job.

If your job can be done with less, find another job.

If your work does not excite you, find another job.

…

And in any of the cases mentioned above, if you don't find it after searching, create it (invent it).

For everyone: do something that requires talent, choose an occupation that provides direction and meaning to people, and choose jobs that are creative, innovative, and require a lot of talent. In short, run away from production jobs like the plague.

Two concepts to consider: interchangeable work and non-interchangeable work. Any work that is interchangeable will change in terms of the job holder and its location (work exported to the east); non-interchangeable work will stay.

Another interesting concept - proximity. If your job requires proximity to the customer, you have a lower risk that it becomes interchangeable or that it can be digitised. There is only one message: specialise in what you do, deliver talent that cannot be digitised, know how not to be interchangeable and develop proximity.

Production work can always be done for less money. Or better, with higher quality and efficiency. Emerging countries constitute the large pool for outsourcing. Companies have already realised that outsourcing (international sub-contracting) improves processes (100% increase in productivity) and lowers costs (75% in salary savings). And they have found that home-sourcing (domestic sub-contracting) improves productivity by 30%.

So, where is your competition? (Yes, your competition!) Answer: Everywhere: they are the people who work from home, the professionals, and the companies that are several thousand kilometres away.

A company employee competes with other people who work for themselves and who want to do work for the same company. We can see them, but soon we will feel them breathing down our necks, and how they can potentially lower payroll costs.

The same thing happens in companies: they not only compete with other companies in the same sector, but with the self-employed who can do the same work, using the same technologies (all have access to the same tools), and with a smaller structure, and therefore more price-competitive. I currently provide training in multinational companies that previously worked with major training companies.

In times of crisis, we get tired of hearing arguments like: *"it's not a good time," "it's not the thing to invest in", "it's risky"* ... When in fact, what they're saying are: *"I am afraid of doing it," "I do not like to do it," "I do not know how to do it"* ...

It isn't the crisis, unemployment, indebtedness, or the market ... it's about us, it's about you. We! You! It's about people who don't believe in themselves and in their possibilities; consequently, they project their distrust of the situation. Crises are largely a lack of confidence (if man can have desires without having doubts about the results, his desires would be fulfilled at once).

I will share with you this quote from Paul Romer: "*A crisis is something that cannot be wasted.*" He also said: "*We all want economic growth, but nobody wants change.*"

Like him, I think a crisis is an opportunity for improvement. They symbolize the need for change, and money loves the rapid pace of change. A crisis is a sign that something new is just around the corner.

The most brilliant mind of the last century, Albert Einstein, said this about crisis: *"Let's not pretend that things will change if we keep doing the same things."* A crisis is the greatest blessing that people and countries can have because it brings progress. Creativity is born out of darkness. Inventions, discoveries and great strategies are born from crises. Whoever overcomes crisis outdoes himself without being "overcome".

Whoever attributes his failures and hardships to a crisis disregards his own talents and has more respect for problems instead of for solutions. The real crisis is the crisis of incompetence. The problem of people and countries is their laziness to find outlets and solutions to their problems. Without crises, there are no challenges, without challenges, life is mere routine, indeed a slow agony.

Let's give the best of ourselves when faced with challenges. It is during a crisis that the best in each person flourishes, because without crisis, every wind is a mere caress. To talk of crisis is to promote it, and to be silent in the crisis is to exalt conformity, instead of working hard at it. Let's get over the only menacing crisis - our tragic unwillingness to overcome it.

Words of wisdom.

4

Why are there Economic Problems?

YOU PROBABLY KNOW that the average employee survives from pay check to pay check. I know it very well because I worked as a director in a bank for ten years. As the third and fourth weeks approach each month, their checking accounts are in the red; employees are waiting for the beginning of the month to recover what they had financially spent. And that goes on month after month.

What a life!

A few years from now, people will be joyously getting into mortgages more than ever before; I say this because the rising costs of mortgages have extended amortisations to 40 years. But if this is not hair-raising enough for anyone, listen to this next thing: after paying half a lifetime to purchase their home, more and more people are getting back into remortgaging their lives, this time by applying for a reverse mortgage so that they'll receive a monthly income to supplement their meagre pensions.

What a legacy!

After a lifetime of hard work, many people have very little money in the bank, with average savings of 30,000 Euros. With that capital and a small Social Security pension, it becomes almost inevitable that the first thing a person does when he retires is to look for work and put as many hours as he can.

Upon retirement, the majority of people leave move away from the middle class to join the lower class. The result is that their retirement years - supposed to be their golden years - transform into a bittersweet period (more bitter than sweet actually) and their purchasing power becomes much lower than what they had during their active years. Where does this working for a whole lifetime lead to?

What a panoramic view!

Given such a scenario, I can now hear your thoughts: "It's not fair." Perhaps it isn't fair, but the facts are there and are the effects of a cause, they're not coincidence or an accident.

This book will address the causes that lead to these kinds of situations and to correct them when it is still possible to do so.

I want you to understand that intensifying your efforts with a "recipe" that does not work will only make the stew worse, so I'm saying that more work or a higher salary are NOT the solutions. This may seem unbelievable but you will soon understand that it is not speed that's missing in the recipe, but the direction in which you're going.

The person who can't make ends meet at the end of the month tends to believe that the ultimate solution to his problems is a higher salary. I don't think so. Why?

Because when a person's salary increases, more taxes are withheld, his spending goes up, and his debt levels increase in proportion to his income. And he's back at square one.

It is obvious that people are in debt because they spend more than they earn, so I'm not sure that increasing one's income would be the solution because it means spending more and hence increasing debt.

They do not need more money; what they need to solve is their habit of spending more than they earn. Yes, you read that correctly.

What they need are two words: financial training. Without this education, a person who earns more money will spend more money or else lose money. In the end, the person who wins the game is not the one who earns more, but one who gets to keep more.

The worst lie that anyone can say is that who he earns more money has more money.

Let's imagine a situation where someone receives a salary increase (this is a risky assumption these days). Months later, that person is more stressed owing to his new job responsibilities and has less free time; furthermore that person spends more, and consequently, he sees the same thing before happening again every month: zero savings. They work hard and spend "hard", borrow money, spend what they have not yet earned... in short, they are the experts at spending. First class shoppers!

Furthermore, their deductions at source have gone up several points. Things have improved for the person only for him to finish in a worse situation. After the promotion, sure, he has a higher income but he also has more responsibility, more taxes, more spending; along with less time, less freedom, less of a life...

Robert Frost, winner of four Pulitzer Prizes, said it impeccably: "*By working faithfully eight hours a day, you may eventually get to be boss and work twelve hours a day.*"

Do you understand why success on the job can translate into a failure? It seems no one realises that.

The solution is not a better salary but a better mentality.

Salaries do not increase. In real terms, they decrease. One only needs to look at the labour market to realise that job offers are not a rare commodity; on the contrary, offers are in great supply. Due to the law of supply and demand, the hourly rate goes lower and lower. Do salaries rise by 20% annually? 10%? Of course not! In real terms with the rate of inflation, wages fall. Why? Because the billions of job applicants in the global market drive down wages.

The entry into the global market of large Asian economies bring in 2.4 million people. Do you honestly think that this won't affect you because you're just a few hours away by plane? Communication satellites are making workers from east and west work next door to each other.

It's happening now: blue-collar workers take a plane to Europe; white-collar workers only require high-speed internet access (they don't have to travel, they just hook into fibre optics). Imagine when you get to work tomorrow, you find that huge labour force in front of your company asking to work for a tenth of what you're paid...somehow, it's going to happen.

No matter what your work is - production, services, manual or intellectual work - sooner or later your work will go virtual, be automated or sub-contracted for less cost and for better performance. There's no turning back: all economic activities will be broken down into parts (processes), and most of them will be digitised (automated) or exported (contracted out) not only to reduce costs. Time to think about how we can improve quality!

Who will win more out of all this? Make no mistake about it. Companies are not the only one who will gain from this, but also consumers (all of us) who will have better goods and services, at better prices.

It wasn't my intention, in the preceding paragraph, to worry you, but rather to invite you to take action. Your best response to this invitation is to not take a shortcut or to huff and puff, but instead to change your way of thinking.

The message is: develop a talent and market it creatively. In a global world, there will be wonderful opportunities for people to change their indifferent or apathetic mindset. But it will be quite a roller for those who think that what's happening at present has nothing to do with them.

The traditional advice is: "*Go to school, get your university degree, find a secure job, work hard all your life, and then retire.*"

It's the worst advice I've ever heard in my life. I shudder just thinking about it. If you can swallow that, would you also believe me if I said I were Elvis Presley?

But, why is such an exotic advice so popular? Look at the people who created this atrocious way of thinking. Imagine how limited their personal finances are. Do you want that for yourself? If not, then don't follow outdated advice.

It's not a good "recipe"; the recipe is bad no matter how good you are at cooking, and the result will taste as lousy.

We've all heard conversations in which someone defends purchasing a flat over renting a flat. The argument is always the same: "If you rent, you're throwing away money, but if you buy, you will always have something that belongs to you." That's right.

Let's apply this now to working. "If you work for others, you're wasting time, but if you work for yourself, you create an asset (a business) which will always be yours." It is also true, but very few people realise it.

Working in exchange for a salary never generates a residual income for you, you will never own anything that you can sell one day, nor can it create wealth for you in the future... The downside of working at a job is that every morning you start from scratch and at night you put zero on your scorecard for the next day. You never own anything, no matter how many years you work at your job, you have nothing in the end because it was never yours to begin with.

A job is a source of income - like "rent" money. You work to receive it but even if you work well at the job, it will never be yours. The problems begin when a company decides not to longer "rent" out a job to a worker.

So if the solution is not getting a better job or earning more pay, what is the solution?

We will get to that later but it is important to realise that *The money code is your passport to financial freedom, you have to see it as your own system of income.* Sounds good, yes? We'll get to that part.

The solution to money problems doesn't lie in money, but in a different mindset.

For a person who receives an amount of money, how many times does he think that it's the end of his troubles? He discovers later that his money troubles are back, and may be even worse than before. The rich are not different from the rest of us, they just have a different mentality and, consequently, have more money. Everyone faces economic challenges and financial problems, the big difference is that the rich face them with a different mentality.

Their financial IQ is what makes them rich, not the money. Intelligence is the ability to make precise distinctions. And financial intelligence allows you to make distinctions in earning and spending in a more refined manner. When you finish reading this book you will be able to see what others do not see.

At the moment, understand that money is the effect of a cause and the cause is always...a type of mentality. If you focus on the effects (the money) but not on the cause (the mind) things will not change. And if they do, they will be short-lived changes. What I'm trying to tell you is that to fix your financial situation, you don't need money; you need a different mindset that will translate into money and much more.

I have discovered that economic problems exist because people ignore the old law of the Process: To be, to do, and to have. Everyone wants something they don't have, but very few realise that to "have" they must first "be" that something they desire. *"First say to yourself what you would be; and then do what you have to do."* (Epictetus.)

To get something, you must first think and feel as if it were already real, and behave as if they're in the process of coming to you. Makes sense to me. For example, if a person wants to have prosperity, in his mind he should be prosperous. And by doing what makes a person successful, he eventually manifests prosperity. To be, to do, to have - and not vice versa as some believe.

Another reason there are financial problems is that people have little or no financial education. Wealthy people have better financial education. Not academic education, but financial education. If you check the list of the richest people in the world, you will see that it wasn't their academic training that made them wealthy. Their attitude did. Their attitude made the difference, and yet every day, legions of people leave home greedy for diplomas (focusing 100% on their aptitude, but 0% on their attitude). Right now I'm holding my head with my hands.

Educational systems prepare us for financial failure. Of course, without malice, intentions don't count, but results do. Let's accept the fact that education, in its traditional sense and as it relates to financial freedom, is nothing. The following is a list of people who dropped out of university (because they weren't taught what they wanted to learn) and you'll see that leaving university did not do them any harm: Richard Branson, Thomas Edison, Agatha Christie, Ted Turner, Mozart, Michael Dell, Steve Jobs, Bill Gates, Henry Ford, Amancio Ortega ...

Paraphrasing Einstein: learning is hampered by education.

Financial education should be taught starting in primary school (Did you study subjects such as "wealth I" and "wealth II" or similar courses? I did not). By financial education I'm not referring to scholarly theories, but to practical laws that anyone can understand and apply in their personal finances.

Educational systems encourage people to study so they can find jobs, but good financial training, when taught, does not mean needing a job. Daniel Pink, visionary writer, wrote in his book, *Free Agent Nation*: "*The educational model of the U.S. is what I call the Thanks-*

giving turkey model: put the kids in the 'oven of formal education' for eleven years until they are well done, then serve them to employers. A few will be cooked for another four years in college." "I feel I have been grilled for too long in the oven." In my case, the faculty of Economics Science trained me to be an employee (white collar), not to be an employer or an entrepreneur (gold collar). And therefore, I used up more years than necessary. I must confess that I have been redeemed.

If you are not earning what you want to earn, there is something about money that you do not know.

The next cause of much financial trouble is that most people are not selling anything except their time. A traditional job consists of selling time based on a contract: 40 hours a week in exchange for a salary. And, I prefer to say this right away, selling your time will not make you achieve financial freedom - it's impossible!. This is the reason why the rich are getting richer while the rest, including the middle class, are getting poorer.

As you know, time is limited: you cannot work beyond 8, 10 or 12 hours a day. There is a limit - you're paid well for your hours but you can't sell more time that you don't have. The rich do not sell their time, they don't need to get employed, but they create systems or businesses to earn income.

Will you open a store with 8, 10 or 12 items on the shelf, and nothing more? Of course not! What a box you'll end up with at the end of the day! That is exactly what happens to those who sell their hours. You have so little to sell, and it is very expensive.

Traditional or conventional work has advantages, no doubt. But there are two significant drawbacks: a) it severely limits freedom and b) potential for economic prosperity is limited.

I was completely uninterested in being employed at some point in my career. Suddenly, I felt I wanted to get rid of my job. I realised that the freedom I was seeking was not going to come from an internal promotion or from a change in jobs, but from a radical change in my way of thinking.

Have not you noticed that those who opt for the safety net are not that enthusiastic and have no sense of purpose?

You can be very good at what you do and have a lousy financial situation because selling your time constitutes a limitation. On the other hand, I do not know any good businessman who is very good at what they do, and barely making it. The reason? Their incomes are not limited. It is not how good you practice your profession that marks your financial success, but how well you handle your limitations and your income. Does anyone realise that?

Another reason that explains why there are economic problems is that like everything in life, money has a price tag. What happens is that too many people think you can get something for nothing. American millionaire Hunt said: *"The secret of success is knowing what you want and being willing to pay the price to get it."*

One: Knowing the "what."

Two: pay the full "price".

Money, like everything, has a price (that not everyone wants to pay). The price of money is paid primarily on: courage, creativity, patience, imagination, passion, discipline, effort, persistence, confidence, willingness to serve, and many other qualities that not everyone is willing to develop. I'll tell you something invaluable: if you want something in life, first find out its price and pay for it gladly. I love paying the price, as it guarantees results.

And finally there are money problems because the problems are, in a way, natural. The truth is that everyone has financial problems, even rich people do; however, the difference lies in the manner of solving them.

Trying to avoid or ignore financial problems does not make them go away, because problems do not resolve themselves. With respect to money, I always say that trying to solve financial problems with money, and not with financial intelligence, is a huge mistake.

Economic problems are not solved with money, but with creativity.

My hope is that this book will break old paradigms about money. I want the reader to understand that money is never the problem; instead the problems are in people's attitudes about money. Trying to achieve a life of freedom and wealth, but handling money the wrong way does not make sense. When you understand this simple principle and apply it, you make a giant step toward freedom and prosperity.

5

The 4 Obstacles to Financial Freedom

AT SOME POINT, you're going to have to make a choice: security or freedom? People who seek security lose freedom and vice versa. Decide on your choice and pay the price, because like I said before, nothing comes free. And here is the problem word: "free." Get away from it.

Those who love security will miss out on opportunities because they go for the easy way out. That shouldn't be your goal. I found an excellent quote by Robert Henri: "*To be free, to be happy, and to be fruitful can only be attained through sacrifice of many common but overestimated things.*"

Honestly, I do not know of quick and easy ways to make money, nor do they interest me because they only spell disaster.

My dear readers, I hope you do not look for the quick and easy path, but if you are, stop reading and give this book to someone else. Thank you and goodbye. And for those who wish to follow me:

If you choose freedom, you will probably make some mistakes. Think about it, it's logical - mistakes are necessary for achieving success. I transform every mistake I make into something good, capitalise on it and use it as a lever. Therefore, withdrawing from mistakes is withdrawing from success or giving up on shake off this absurd fear of error. Winston Churchill had it right: *"Success consists of going from failure to failure without losing enthusiasm."* I would even prefer to make mistakes in things I like doing, than correcting mistakes in what I detest.

People who avoid mistakes are avoiding success.

When you start something new, mistakes are inevitable. Someone said that if you want to succeed you should "double your error rate" because it's from these errors that you learn. I hope I have convinced you of the necessity that making mistakes is vital. Find your "memorable error", your pivotal point and revolutionize your life. There are other "worlds" and they are here, available.

For an employee, errors are to be avoided. For an entrepreneur, errors are a necessary part of the process.

Taking risks means having the opportunity to win, not to lose.

If you choose security, you deprive yourself of financial freedom because the two - security and financial freedom - are incompatible. Not taking risks leads to a small life. *"If you do not risk anything, you risk everything,"* said Geena Davis, an actress. A smart lady. I know it's an important choice, I myself have made it many times. I have found, nevertheless, that security has more followers - so much more - than freedom has. At school, we were taught to play it safe; unfortunately it was an obstacle to learning.

I did not see the relationship between what I studied and reality.

Security or freedom? Go with what you want. I believe that financial freedom is more important than job security. One is real, the other, a fantasy. Make the choice and you take responsibility; pay the price of your choice, and you won't see yourself as a victim, nor will you complain about your situation, whatever it is.

But let's turn to the barriers to financial freedom:

The first obstacle are the beliefs that limit us. Many beliefs are a heavier burden than a mortgage, in fact they act like "mental mortgages." I think it's better to be encumbered by a mortgage loan in the bank than have mental limitations that we impose on ourselves. The former has an expiration date, whereas beliefs, in principle, do not.

This book seeks to debunk common beliefs about money based on fear. I will not go deeper into this topic because I have written enough, but I will say that fear is the biggest barrier - collectively and individually.

The second obstacle is the complacent attitude to living within one's comfort zone, through the force of habit. We have phobias about effort. The only people who want an immediate change are babies with wet diapers. Many people feel good when they're within their comfort zone. Sad, isn't it?

We should be clear that our personal finances will improve only when we improve ourselves. Yes, effort is uncomfortable, but it is more uncomfortable to continue experiencing financial problems! In a changing world, not adapting to changes is too risky for those who seek comfort.

This is what's comfortable and easy: *"insufficient pay, an infinite mortgage, irresponsible spending"* - these no longer work. Recycle yourself.

The third obstacle are bad financial habits. The average person looks for immediate financial gratification and does not follow a mid-term and long term financial strategy. Financially, he lives day-to-day. He earns, spends what he earns without saving, and worse: does not invest. He depends on a sole source of income over which he has no control. He spends more than he earns, and even spends future earnings. He is indebted for life without creating other sources of income that would pay for his obligations, offering himself luxuries without considering his cash flow.

In short, he wants a lifestyle that he has not yet earned. It's time to re-examine these habits.

Whatever your current situation, the fact is that the way you think and act have led you exactly to where you are today. Face it: your bank balance is not the result of chance, but is the result of some habits. If you want to create a different balance, you will need to get rid of old habits and replace them with good ones.

The fourth obstacle is the lack of a financial education. Everyone handles money every day, but few are prepared to do it correctly. A good financial education is not a luxury but a prime necessity. And if you think it's not, just ask people who bought financial products they did not understand. What they purchased turned out to be worthless.

The fact that it is not taught in school does not mean it is not necessary. The days when a university degree will prepare you for the rest of life in the professional milieu are now history. Today, the amount of information to humans doubles every eighteen months (Moore's Law); back in the year 1500, however, if you were reading a book every week for four years, you would have finished reading all the books in the world and you shall have covered the whole knowledge of mankind.

Do the calculations. Re-learning your life is the only way to avoid being left out of the economic game. It is no longer worth hiding behind a college degree because like I said, although it is necessary it does not make a big difference. It does not guarantee a job, and it does not ensure financial freedom.

Continuous training is a priority. And for those who think this seems like an expensive option, a luxury, how about trying ignorance?

Here's an aphorism: Your income can grow as far as you want it to grow but no more (re-read this line - it is the essence of this book).

6

Retirement, the Financial Future that is Uncertain

STATISTICS REVEAL that the greatest fear people have is running out of money after retirement. And if we don't do anything about it, it will happen to many when they retire.

The idea of "working hard for a lifetime leads to a golden retirement" is not realistic; worse still, it's a hoax. Hopefully, this book will prevent you from the great disappointment that awaits my generation at the age of retirement. If we still have years ahead of us, we can prepare ourselves in avoiding disaster. People can't improvise, but they can certainly prepare.

I found statistics that sent shivers down my spine. In the world's richest country - USA - when people turn 65; that is, when they reach retirement age, 1% of them are considered **very** wealthy, 4% are financially comfortable, 5% continue working way beyond retirement out of necessity, 54% survive thanks to family help, and for the rest - 36% - they've gone off to a better life, as the saying goes. Let me point out that only 5% are well-positioned, while the rest have not resolved their retirement issues. And, they either have to work or depend on their savings, because the average income of a retired American is $7,000 a year. That's giving you something to survive in a miserable manner, but not to live fully.

Wait...it gets even worse.

Let's go to another large country - Russia. It's an emerging economy. Did you know that the first thing a retired Russian does is to look for work? His savings are so fragile that he can't afford anything, nor can he afford an anxiety attack. His meagre pension (about 100 Euros a month on average) forces him to work while he's still alive. You wouldn't want to find yourself in that situation, would you?

And at what age are we going to retire? Those who know say that retirement will be postponed to a later age - 70 and perhaps older. The State is already encouraging people to voluntarily postpone their retirement (although hardly anyone is taking the hint) so that their pension amounts can be increased by 3% for every year worked beyond age 65.

How long are we going to live? With each passing day, life expectancy increases by five and a half hours (thanks to medical progress). Another thing we know now is that there is no limit to life, we have no programming or a biological clock in our genes to enable us to prevent reaching the age of a hundred or two hundred years. We're living longer.

Someone will have to subsidise the huge social costs of a long and massive retirement of people (the trend for half of this century and beyond is that there are more Europeans over age 60 than those aged 20 and younger). One important detail as well: in developed countries, they are registering negative birth rates. The UN says that by 2050, Spain will have the third oldest population in the world (after Japan and Italy). The million dollar question is...hold on... Who's going to pay for so many retirement parties? The disturbing reply: maybe no one.

The Social Security payment system has become something similar to a Ponzi pyramid scheme: the last ones who get in shall pay for those already inside the pyramid. Financial pyramids, as we've seen a thousand times, finally crumble when no one is coming in to finance the rest of the members. And what is happening is that there are no increases in active contributions to pay the pensions of the growing mass of retirees.

Let's tell a story. In the 1940's, when 65 was established as the retirement age, life expectancy was 63 years. This meant that a person worked a lifetime; today, however, with the present life expectancy, retiring at 65 is now an outdated idea. In the coming years, we have to hope that the retirement age will be updated to 70 years - more or less - to bring it more in line with new standards of living.

Did your father and his Social Security cheques take care of you? How do you know? The state pension system is not intended to perform the functions of a retirement plan (although everyone understands it as such). In fact, it is set up in such a way that it serves as a complementary arrangement to your own retirement plan, which is your responsibility. I regret to say that this has led self-deception. When something as vital as our retirement income is concerned, I don't think anyone should delegate it to anyone, improvise upon it, or trust in luck.

The goal of enjoying a golden retirement has turned into a myth.

In short, nobody knows if Social Security can guarantee a pension or medical coverage for us. It's something you know in time, but this subject, in my opinion, is too important to leave to chance. It is foolish to think that someone will solve our personal financial problems. I'd rather look after my own finances now, before I learn at some future time that no one will do it for me.

What's the solution to the public pension system? There are two very unpopular solutions which can delay and worsen the prognosis by pension experts. One, extending the legal retirement age; and two, enlarging the basis for calculating contributions, from the current 15 years to 35 years.

Dreaming of retiring with 1 million Euros or Dollars in savings would be great, but for a person who has been employed throughout his life, this is merely a fantasy, a fantasy that is impossible to turn into reality.

Let's do some number-crunching: if an average person earns 24,000 Euros annually (2,000 per month), he would make 1,000,000 Euros throughout his working life. Do the calculations, many people spend a million and a half Euros. Yes, all make a million at the end of their working lives, so do you. But we have to pay taxes, eat, buy clothes, and pay for housing ... so how do we save 100% of our earnings? It's quite clear that you can't retire with a million in the bank. The numbers don't add up.

Let's look into more complicated numbers. I call into the stage the depreciation diva: inflation. Yes, yes, it's the sustained fall of the value of money. Now, has your salary also increased proportionately? If the answer is "no", and I bet it is, you are less solvent, to put it in a friendly way.

Retirement: it is the entry threshold of the middle class to lower class.

How can this happen? It's the lack of a financial education, no doubt. I hope you understand that a financial education is of prime and utmost necessity. I imagine you're nodding your head in silence.

Changes in some segments of the labour market (temporary jobs, discontinued occupations and professions, volatile contracts, low pay ...) will be such that the next generation cannot aspire to save for retirement and they will have to continue working after retirement.

There's this joke which probably isn't a joke: job is the acronym for *Just On Broke*. Swallow that.

Another thing.

Retirement should not be equated with freedom because it implies that you don't like your occupation, or even that you find it disgusting. "*Most people perform essentially meaningless work. When they retire, that truth is borne upon them"*. Brendan Francis' words. I concur. Most retirees would have done things they wanted to do. And what this book offers is to get you organised financially so that your active years become your ideal retirement: plenty of time and money and just when you can benefit from them more.

7

Do you Live in a World that No Longer Exists?

LET me begin this section with a quote from Eric Hoffer, a philosopher: "*In times of change, learners inherit the Earth, while the learned find themselves beautifully equipped to live in a world that no longer exists."* Isn't it disturbing?

Let's look at the environment. This is part of what is happening:

I was born and raised in the industrial era, now an extinct era. Today in the West, this era is almost a memory and yet so many people still behave as though nothing had changed. It's like looking at an account in pesetas each time it is paid or charged in Euros. The industrial age is now a reality in the East; it is not the case in the West where we're living in the information era (from which consciousness springs).

At this point, information is abundant, it either doesn't cost much or is free. Never before has the price of wealth been so affordable. Land, factories, or capital are no longer necessary to make money; what's necessary is valuable information. (I think of myself as an info-preneur because knowledge is the core of my profession). Today the economy is being shaken by a puzzling occurrence because we are what I call a "hinge generation"; that is, hinged between two eras: the industrial and information eras. Since only a few are aware of it, they're still applying the old rules of the industrial era to the information age, and hence are losing out in the financial game.

- In the agricultural era, land was wealth.
- In the industrial era, capital was wealth.
- In the information era, information is wealth.
- In the knowledge era, wealth will be at a higher awareness level.

Regarding information, I will say that data will be digitised. What does this mean exactly?

Rest assured that if something can be digitised, it will be sooner or later. Any information can be digitised (conversion of atoms into bits). Our generation is the hinge generation; that is, we were born "analog" but we must be converted to "digital", and believe me, at the mentality level it is not as simple as changing a typewriter for a computer. Or replacing an analog TV with digital TV.

My fellow "analogues", this message is for you: we have little time, guys, so I would make peace with the new technologies. I believe that even if we don't realise that it is a digital world, a particular person (say you) and a company (say Microsoft) have the same capability to use the same computer tools. Are you going to use or disregard your capability which is equal to the capability of a large multinational?

But:

Knowledge is more than information. It is the next level. Having information does not imply having knowledge. Although knowledge is based on information, information is not knowledge, since possessing data does not imply its adequate use nor does it guarantee that its possession in "memory" will be incorporated into thought processes. Moving from an information society to a knowledge society will require learning to separate dispensable information from the expendable, and above all incorporating them from experience.

This has only just begun. Complexity has come and has settled among us. Technophobes, you have no chance. Sorry to say. I hear some people complaining: May everything return to normal! They do not understand, this is normal!

The new currency is called knowledge, and people are rich or poor according to their degree of knowledge.

Nobody knows what the future will be, but we all suspect that it will be quite different from what we imagine now. I found a disturbing quote about it: *"The factory of the future will have only two employees: a man and a dog. The man will be there to feed the dog. The dog will be there to keep the man from touching the equipment"*; it's a quote from Warren G. Bennis, a visionary and adviser to U.S. presidents.

Look, good information can make you rich, and poor information can make you poor. It's not such a strange idea. Beliefs are already in the making. Therefore, the stress is on the need for financial training and learning during our lifetime. My parents taught me from an early age that ignorance is the worst kind of poverty as it invariably leads to spiritual and material poverty.

Speaking of material poverty: the number of people living on less than a dollar a day is 1,100 million. And how many live on less than a dream during their entire life? Much more, there's another kind of poverty ... I am thinking of a quotation I read some time ago written by Harry Kemp who said: *"The poor man is not he who is without a cent, but he who is without a dream"*.

You cannot play the money game, but you can lose it.

Like it or not, when it comes to money, we will have to learn to earn it, spend it, and invest it. We all play, some play better, some play worse ... Are you winning your game? If you do not feel that you are winning, put this book on your bedside table. Most people are losing the game right now, not for lack of opportunities, but for their ignorance about the rules of the game. How can they win the game without having the slightest idea of the rules? Congratulate yourself, this book provides sufficient guidance on how to win the money game. Very few people know the "ABCs" of money - but you're about to discover them.

The rules are now different in the new economic environment, and those who play by the old rules get left out of the game. Problems arise when people ignore or violate the rules. For example, the concept of "employment as a means of making a living" is stale. It refers to the industrial era. Yes, a job is an out-of-date approach and applying it to a global world in the information age generates more disadvantages than advantages.

Message: the only problem about being employed is the high price to pay.

Those who adapt to changes in the new economic era can take advantage of them and enjoy life more. The term "job position" has lost its meaning because the "work place" is no longer a determining factor (outsourcing is only the tip of the iceberg of a broader phenomenon: globalization). By contrast, telecommuting or remote working will replace the outdated concept of "office work". Down with the gray carpeted cubicle partitions! We are not fish, we don't want fish tanks!

Definition of Telecommuting: "working from the sofa at home." Cool, isn't it? All you'll ever need: a PC, a wifi connection, a mobile phone, and a good steaming cup of tea, and you've got it all there on the table.

It is the result of the information society that makes intensive use of communication technologies. Is that something you want? Then I welcome you to one of the emerging patterns of recruitment based on results and self-responsibility. The teleworker is more efficient, more motivated, more autonomous, has more time for the family, and more freedom. And he has less stress, doesn't wear to have stuffy ties, has fewer bosses, fewer "heavy-duty" colleagues, and doesn't have to travel everywhere. The company that hires him benefits from lower overheads, in addition to "buying" results, not buying the person's time.

You already heard me saying that in the information era, job security simply does not exist. If someone ever thought that a secure job is more important than financial freedom, I will say that any job is safe until the day that person is fired. A salary can provide you with a sum of money, yes, but it cannot give you security. Security is a superstition that lies deep in the dreaming mentality of man.

Secure employment is a thing of the past. Gradually, all conditions relating to job security will be subject to what the market dictates. Perhaps there are still "risk-free or iron-clad jobs" out there, but every day, when more people lose their traditional jobs, they will constitute the competition for these so-called "risk-free" jobs. There will be many applicants for these jobs held by those who want to preserve their own jobs against competing applicants.

"Security" is now a fossil, and the carbon-14 test does not tell lies!

In the old economy wages increased; in the new economy, they are going down. Since 1950, the world's economies were "going over" - were overflowing; but starting in 2007, the world's economies have been shrinking." Since 1980, globalization has reduced salaries by 7% in industrialized countries (source: IMF).

Inflation has also significantly reduced salaries. In the last 25 years, the global workforce quadrupled and will register a 40% growth by 2050. The law of supply and demand says: more supply, lower wages. This phenomenon is known in the streets as the precariousness of jobs, low wage brackets, trashy contracts, etc.

What are the governments doing about it? They're granting subsidies - which is the politics of compassion, and that translates into "bread today, hunger tomorrow" programmes - programmes that keep the poor in poverty. I really do not think that subsidies put an end to poverty.

And what about foreign multinationals? They are offered juicy tax breaks so they don't pack their bags and leave...but I'll save my comments. What about the workers, how do they face up to the situation? The OECD recognizes that workers have made concessions on wages just to keep their jobs. And I wonder, is this all we are able to do?

Job security, office work, position, guaranteed retirement, guaranteed health care, permanent job - all these concepts are increasingly getting blurred...and vague.

Governments seek to increase the working week but do not increase wages. Companies also increase the amount of work, but do not increase salaries. In short, salaries are going down.

There was a time when having children was an assurance of receiving of financial support in our old age, and this model worked for centuries. Today, there is continuing doubt. The reverse is true. These days, children can barely keep up financially. The new group of active workers who earn less than a thousand a month are slaves to their jobs, are entrenched in their mortgages, and totally supported by their parents - who must also support a crowd of people entering retirement. How can a few people help so many if they themselves need a lot of help?

Take note: The generation that will succeed the present generation will be the first - but not the last - who will say that their parents were better off than them! (from "going further" to "going less further").

In short, we live in a new era with new rules, although many are still behaving as before; that is, playing the rules of a world that no longer exists. Meanwhile, jobs are migrating, the middle class is declining, wages are falling, the ability to save is evaporating, the level of poverty is going up, household debt is on the rise, the number of people working past retirement is growing, and retirement pensions are in limbo. Does anyone realise what is happening?

8

Globalization is Here to Stay

THE MEDIA often talk of oneness, that the world is a united entity - but what does it mean? To me, it is complex and it will remain with us. I have the impression that we "ain't seen nothin" yet", and later, we will all have to learn to live together in a super complex and changing world.

Intelligence is the ability to make precise distinctions. What oneness conveys is the impression of a "flat mind", it is one-dimensional. The multi-dimensionality of the complexity cannot be understood if people don't know how to refine it in order for them to understand the new world.

In my opinion, Europe has experienced a 50-year hiatus in the twentieth century, an exceptional stage that doesn't guarantee the welfare state in the future; because, among other things, it never existed in the world - except in North America and in Japan. I rather think that we are now leaving a bubble and returning to the real world. The stage that began in 1950 characterised by sustained growth and guaranteed welfare (the largest economic boom in history) has come to an end, whether we like it or not.

The "culture of merit" is self-indulgent. It's weak. The welfare state has encouraged an accommodating society and has also weakened. We have given the government more power over our lives. I think it's time to stop demanding for rights and assume our duties instead. We should embrace the "culture of effort" if we want to maintain our standard of living. And it is impossible to maintain a standard of living without exerting the effort. Jose Ugarte, head of the mega Mondragon cooperative, said: "*People have no idea how much they need to change if they want to keep what they have. They do not realise how fast this is happening.*"

If our young people want to match the standard of living of their parents, they must put on the right "batteries." And if they want to improve, I fear that a simple change of batteries will not suffice. Fortunately, they did not have a world war to recover from, but if they're facing an economic war, they must liberate their conscience and make the same effort as their fathers did to come out ahead and succeed.

Everyone to action station!

For too long, too many people think that the state would take care of them. They expect the government to solve their financial problems. The stark reality is that we, and nobody else, are responsible for our own financial well-being. The solution to our economic problems will not come from the state, which is too busy counting its money, but from our financial IQ. You cross your arms perhaps in indifference, but you know it's true.

Globalization has come and is now part of our life. It is the effect of communication channels connecting all of the world's economies. It's as if the crystal vase broke - the crystal vase where 1.260 million live (North America, Europe and Japan) and who were separated from the rest of the world. But now that it's broken, they have to live with 5,450 million other people. In the short term, globalization will be traumatic, especially for the minority who see their once privileged status crumbling. On the other side of the planet, many are beginning begin to dream about escaping poverty and entering the middle class.

So is globalization good or bad? It depends.

For those who lose a job in the West, it is bad, for those who live in the East, it is a good thing. The World Bank has warned that the redistribution of work in the world market will be costly for the rich countries. Europeans and Americans can take advantage of globalization; but it is also true that not everyone will do so. There will be those who will win and those who will lose the money game. Talent does not have jurisdiction in the global environment, but those who compete on price will see the deterioration of their finances. Of course if we add all the effects, I believe that globalization is good for all humanity. The bad thing is that we now have to pay the price of "unification."

Another thing. Moving forward with the excessive burden of countless government administrations is embarrassing (did you know that a Spanish government worker has more staff than other developed countries?) If we add low competitiveness caused by a progressive reduction of our productivity, the resulting scenario is nothing to celebrate about.

Still, I'm observing what's happening in the world and I see two dimensions (on the mental level, not at the geographical level): in the first, there's a crisis and in the other, the opposite. There are economies in recession and there are economies that are emerging. The question is whether you're going to convert your personal financial situation into an emerging personal financial situation or into a recessionary personal financial situation, regardless of what's happening in your immediate environment.

Now you will listen to everything, depending on who you talk to. The uniqueness of the pessimistic news is that it's not reliable because this multidimensionality is ignored. They paint a "flat" world where nothing good happens. The media are getting bored.

I watched a documentary on TV about a surreal but true story: an American employee in Tucson loses his job which was "exported" to Shanghai. Consequently, a Chinese person gets the new job, makes it to the middle class, buys a small apartment in a horrible building, but no matter, it will be his home.

Meanwhile, as the American could no longer afford to pay his mortgage, his house is repossessed by the bank and was auctioned off. He plants a tent in a place where people are broke like him and they all put up a fight for a square meter of living space. This kind of situation is widespread.

In Shanghai, at this time, an entire plane has been chartered, transporting Chinese investors who come to Tucson to attend a mega auction of hundreds of foreclosed homes. The boss of the Chinese man who got his job from the American is in this group and he's bidding, bidding, bidding...he finally buys the foreclosed house.

The U.S. bank makes peace, it neither wins nor loses. Who will use the house? The Chinese boss's son will use the house when he grows up and studies at a U.S. university where one day he will work (and maybe even get to see his job exported overseas). The Tucson house has a new owner, and work has been transferred away from the continent. Everything is equal yet different. Life goes on.

The opinion in the West is that to defend jobs with low added value is a big mistake. Protecting these positions presumes an agony that will end sooner or later, and that a more than probable situation will result like exporting employment in the Orient.

Meanwhile, the strong resistance compounds the problem by consuming valuable time and energy; we invest by reacting and creating other sources of wealth - this would solve the problem in the medium term. Ultimately, taking cover behind a job over months or years will generate a terrible problem among the unemployed.

The more you think about it, the worse it looks.

The solution? Be really strong. Workers should train to change industry or sector, or even to change professions for the sake of changing their mentality. This will help them understand the need to make the transition to the economic environment, encouraging them to create their own source of income ...

I'm being very clear on this point: I'm saying that things will never be like they were before.

9

Financial Intelligence and Financial Freedom

WHEN YOU READ THIS TITLE, you may sigh and feel the emotion of a yearning unfulfilled. I would like to accompany you in fulfilling it. Let me first introduce two concepts:

The first concept: Financial Intelligence (F.I.)

It is basically the concept of stopping to work for money, to stop selling your time and instead, to create a multiple income system that works for you. In summary, FI means you stop getting up every day to go to work - to a job. The lack of FI is to be blamed for the fact that despite working long and hard, people do not earn enough to cope with economic fairness.

There is nothing wrong with a job, except that the majority do not wish to be employees. (To those who are content with what they do, and are satisfied with the remuneration they receive in return, I will say that this is not their book, then can give it as a gift to a friend, and they will surely find one who will appreciate it.)

For the others, continue reading. I wrote this book for those who desire: a) more freedom, and b) more prosperity.

I believe in the need for multiple and variable sources of income, most of them passive. I shall explain the concept of "passive income" below. For now, let's say it is a financially smart move to diversify one's sources of income.

When financial intelligence is lacking, what happens is that many people expect the government to step in and solve their financial problems. With this mindset, you are giving the State control over your personal power and freedom.

The second concept: Financial Freedom (F.F)

This has nothing to do with an amount of money you have, it has to do with the amount of time in your hands. F.F. is measured by calculating the number of months you can maintain the same standard of living if you should stop working. The more months there are, the more you will be financially free.

Everyone should have funds to cover 6 or 12 months of expenses. But I can actually confirm that this is not the case. You'd be surprised how many people are living on a month's salary - it's the road to bankruptcy, nothing more. F.F. consists of not worrying about where the next euro or dollar will come from; in short, it's the time when you need neither income nor a single euro or dollar.

Imagine that you have a certain amount in the bank which gives you the luxury of not working 1 or 2 years without lowering your standard of living. How would you feel? I'm sure you'll feel relaxed when your boss calls you into his office, or when the announcement is made that there will be a series of relocations and job redundancy schemes.

Allow yourself to accept the idea that intelligent people are programmed to obtain better and various incomes each year. They seek to improve the incomes of previous years in percentages; for example, by 10%, 20%, 30%, 40%, 50% or more. Of course this is only possible if you have variable sources of income. Generally, payrolls don't grow beyond the rate of inflation. As you know, a salary has a ceiling - and unless it is supplemented by variable incomes, a job will not spare anyone from being poor.

Millionaire minds have only two rules:

Rule # 1 Do not limit your income.

Rule # 2 Never forget Rule # 1.

Entrepreneurs think in these terms: apply an annual income budget then do what is necessary to achieve that figure. People can be "programmed" for monthly or annual income amounts. Many are mentally programmed for low amounts year after year (they never double or triple). I believe that many earn an average of 30% less than what they could cover because a higher figure "scares" them. If this is your case, you can change this internal programming and fix your income: Choose how you will win!

Each one earns the salary he attaches to himself, and accepts it, regardless of the real value of their work which can be much higher.

I can "hear" your thoughts: *"That's impossible."*

We use the word "impossible" too frequently, and no one really knows what it means. "Impossible" is something that has not been done until someone does it. Period. *"The world is moving so fast these days that the man who says it can't be done is generally interrupted by someone doing it."* I am quoting E. Hubbard. What to you is impossible is being made possible by someone right now.

Here's an example of how much the world is changing within a short time: in 1990, there was only one web page on the Internet. In 1994, there were 10,000 pages. Hard to believe? Today there are about 2.7 million pages with 5 million pages being created daily. The same has happened with e-mail: in 1992, governments, scientific institutions, and universities had only one email account. Today they cannot be counted, because a quarter of mankind (1.6 billion people) use the Internet.

In addition to Financial Intelligence (FI) you will need to develop Emotional Intelligence (EI).

Warren Buffet said that for an investor to be a good investor, he must control his emotions. I totally agree. For me, EI complements FI. Developing EI implies developing self-control: discipline, confidence, acceptance and rejection of error, limitless patience, deferred instead of immediate gratification. As these behaviours are rarely developed, most can't improve their financial situation.

Study the equation:

Financial Freedom = Financial Intelligence + Emotional Intelligence

Where's the conventional training? ...

And the IQ? ...

And luck?...

They're found nowhere, because they don't count toward financial freedom.

Because school does not teach us to manage neither our emotions nor our money, it follows that we are not prepared for financial freedom. Do you want proof?

Here it is: "The paradox of school grades," states: "In any school and class, the most intelligent, or those with top marks will not necessarily be the richest in class." Isn't this thought annoying? Think about it, please.

Key point: it is not what you know (aptitude), but who you are ! (attitude).

What is intelligence? It is the ability to make precise distinctions - distinctions that are increasingly refined and more subtle. Let's make them for income purposes.

There are 3 different kinds of income:

1 Active income

Requires your presence and work every time you earn - again and again

2 Passive income

Requires your presence and work at first, but then it almost automatically produces on its own

3 Investment earnings

They never require your presence; your money works for you automatically

A financially intelligent person:

- Diversifies his sources of income in these three categories.
- He knows that having a single income is a risk that must be remedied.
- He carries out a business, forms a customer base, earns sales commissions...from his home and in his spare time.

Since time is limited, part of the income has to be passive income; that is, once it's created, it automatically replicates. For example, a customer base is a passive source of income because once generated, will produce benefits indefinitely.

It's obvious that a financially intelligent person does not sell only his time. He also sells his own products and services, or that of others. Asset income and salaries are the most common forms of what a person can earn, but they cannot provide prosperity or freedom. They cannot give what they cannot give, by their very nature. The incomes of wealthy-minded people are passive incomes, as well as incomes from their business and investments (which are not generated by selling one's time).

A financially savvy person solves his financial problems with imagination, not with money. He doesn't get into debt, does not withdraw from his savings, or if he does withdraw, puts the money back.

To work on a commission basis or on producing results provides variable incomes. He treats himself to luxuries only after he creates a revenue stream, but not before this income stream has been established.

Respect rule # 1 on how to get rich:

Never put a limit on how much income you can make. And because you know that a pay check is limited, you wouldn't be interested in making your pay check your only source of income.

The reality is that almost everyone thinks that having a job and having a boss are normal, that they're part of life. I think they are common, yes, but they shouldn't be. It does not seem normal for someone to tell you what to do and how to do it or with whom, or to tell you where you will work, what your daily schedule is, when to relax during your work day, what vacation dates you'll be taking and how much money you'll make. Sorry, but what happens very frequently in our lives does not seem normal to me. Just thinking about it makes my ears ring and makes my blood pressure rise.

Timothy Ferriss in his brilliant book "*The Four-Hour Work Week*" writes: "*Working eight hours a day is a social convention and is an anachronistic legacy of measuring results in volume. How is it possible that everyone in the world needs exactly 8 hours to do their job? It's impossible. The 9 to 5 schedule is arbitrary.*"

I even think that if there was no schedule to follow, any work could be done in less time. In the new economy, people will not be paid for their hours, but for the results they produce. My dear reader, prepare yourself. If you're asked what you do, don't describe what you actually do, but mention what results you've obtained – your achievements.

Concentrate on getting results, not on being busy.

If you search and keep searching, you will find a law or statement with a surprising twist. For instance, I found Parkinson's Law which states: "*Work expands to fill the time available for its completion.*" The more time you have available to do something, you lose more time not doing it. This means, if we shorten the work day, we would complete more tasks.

Trivial tasks (80%) would be on one side and we would focus on the vital ones (20%). Results would improve! Now I understand what the Zen saying meant: less is more.

Do you want to know the secret on how to do more?

Have less time (not more, as you might think).

Yes, you read that correctly. For example, a student is more productive during the week before the exam than if he had a month to study. And an employee completes more tasks in the last half hour of the day than during the entire day. It's plain math.

When I was a bank employee, I discovered that my wealthiest clients had a very different way of thinking than my non-wealthy clients. They had grand thoughts while the others had small thoughts. Both the wealthy and not wealthy have similar brains, the only difference is their mentality.

They make use of their minds in a distinctive way, and this is the reason why their personal situations are also different. Their particular and distinct mindsets hold distinct beliefs that lead to attitudes, habits and behaviours, all of which create different economic realities.

There are many reasons for this difference, but one reason is that the rich (the Forbes list of the world's richer) are aware of the Money Code and use it fully. I hope that with the publication of this book, I unravel and reveal the Code to you.

For now, both groups show differences at the level of conscious thought and unconscious beliefs. The only difference between a prosperous person and one who is not is that the former creates his economic reality consciously and deliberately, while the second does it unconsciously. The thing they have in common is they create it (because somehow, one way or another, human beings do create).

At the conscious level, all people desire economic well-being, but at the unconscious level, they nurture limitations, making such limitations thrive: unjustified fears, impossible assumptions, addictive beliefs, pernicious habits, prejudices,...

Pause for a moment from your reading and ask yourself how you're going to read things if you don't turn off your inner limitations.

The problem is that many do not even know that they have a problem because of their unconscious beliefs (and hence are invisible). Today we know that with its programmed patterns, the unconscious rules our lives. And luckily, financial coaching makes it possible to reveal all these internal barriers to wealth.

In short, when someone is employed, he is "renting out" his intellect for a wage, whereas an entrepreneur puts his mind to work for himself, and considers it his "safety deposit box" (take a quick look at this book's cover - it's the perfect metaphor for the millionaire mind).

Entrepreneurs cannot afford the luxury of renting out to others, they need it for themselves!

10

What They Didn't Tell You About Money

SIT NEXT TO ME, I'll tell you one thing I proved during my financial freedom seminars: none of the participants has had a financial education. Not one. If there's one thing, people who come to me say: *"No one taught me anything about money and how to earn it. Neither my parents nor the school showed me how to get ahead financially."*

It's a shame because we all use money everyday. With the passing of time, these people felt they had to do something about it and decided to seek help and learn the necessary lessons.

Countries should not worry about their production systems, they should do something with their education systems. Maybe it would improve the country's quality. Schemes using the formal education approach in the West are one or two centuries behind. An eternity.

Entering a school today is equal to what it was like 100 years ago. The photograph of the head of state has changed and the walls have been given a fresh coat of paint. Go into a bank branch today and compare it to what it was like 50 years ago and you'll see the difference. Where is the evolution in the educational system?

Does anyone really think that we are adequately preparing our kids for the world they're going to be facing? Daniel H. Pink - note this name down - wrote that the main problem is the *"irrelevance of educational systems to new needs."* The educational system "plants" the seed of employment in the minds of young people; each year it produces a promotional harvest of future employees.

How many rich employees do you know? Me, I know of no one. Does anyone realise this?

A physician and author of numerous bestsellers that were turned into movies, Michael Crichton wanted to study to become a writer. He enrolled at Harvard where he started getting poor grades. Discouraged, he tested his teacher by presenting her with a famous essay written by George Orwell which he submitted as his own. His teacher did not notice the plagiarism nor did he approve it. Disappointed, he decided to write for himself.

His key: intensive use of imagination.

The more you read, the more you realise that many of the financial problems that adults have could be prevented with a good financial education. But schools don't teach students how to manage money matters. In the elementary and higher levels of the educational system, qualifications constitute the measure of academic success. They are, however, useless in real, practical life. To make things worse, programs are way backwards: reward memory instead of moving forward - penalise imagination - all such programs are the reason why people today are studying in a world that does not exist.

Yes, the world we're studying in no longer exists. If you do not believe me, look at a political map of Europe developed 30 years ago and compare it with a current one. For me, I'm suspended in a sort of political geography exam. Luckily, my clients do not ask me what the capital cities of Europe are. Nor do they ask me what grades I got in my drawing or gymnastics courses.

I am the product - the fruit - of an educational system that made me memorise the list of Gothic kings. To this day, I have not been able to fit this information in any of my casual or informal conversations. The subject has never come up. Should I forget it?

Let's face it, what we learned in school will not help us to be rich or free.

This may seem incredible, but it's true: we are trained to avoid mistakes. We were taught that mistakes are bad, which is far from the truth. Making errors is normal - and necessary - for learning. In fact, a millionaire recommended that people who want to succeed should "double their error rate." Then I realised that I was making "too little" mistakes in life and thereafter I decided to double my error rate. More learning mistakes, more success.

Now I know that when I make mistakes, I can find the right path. It is advisable to err on different things each time, but don't repeat the same mistakes! To say it in a few words, the formula for success is: in learning, errors made exponentially would equal inevitable success.

Financial education makes a big difference in economic success.

To earn double or triple the amount you want, it isn't necessary to know or work two or three times more. Does this make sense to you? I'll explain it.

For example, a director of a company can earn two times more than his colleagues. He isn't smarter than them, nor does he know more than them all together. On the contrary. But he has certain abilities that the rest have not developed.

Another example: in Olympic competitions, third and fourth places may represent a negligible difference - thousandths of a second - but it's enough of a difference so that the fourth placer does not make it to the podium.

I'm not saying not to undergo training, or to not send your kids to university. I'm just saying that these days, a career or a Master's Degree does not guarantee financial freedom. These things are necessary, but it is no longer sufficient to have an academic title; especially when higher education in our country amounts to the lowest profitability levels among developed countries, according to the OECD.

What does make a difference is a strategy that is far from the widely-known strategy of "Study, get a degree, find a secure job, work hard, save, and retire with a pension."

This is a paradigm that's "full of dandruff" (it would be shiny if it were true).

No, it doesn't seem to be a sophisticated approach; worse, it no longer works. It's an approach that's doomed to fail, end up a disaster.

Graduates today learn more than ever but are making less money than before…This is why a good academic education is necessary, but it does not guarantee financial success.

But:

In a world of change, constant self-training is needed so as not to fall behind. If you want to succeed in your field, you have to constantly train in your field. For this you will have to "draw up" your own study plan or "curriculum". Do you understand why Mark Twain said, "*I never let school interfere with my education*"?

Is Europe the cult continent? In history books and in museums, perhaps, not in universities.

Let's see how things work here and on the other side of the Atlantic. The Nobel Prizes can help clarify this point. What can be deduced from the statistics is that the Nobel winners trained in American universities earn more - by a huge margin - than those trained in European universities - in a ratio of seven to one.

The reason? In the United States, 2.9% of the GDP is allocated to higher education while in Europe, it is 1.5%. That's half. It is not by chance that technical and scientific disciplines take the lead.

China now produces twice more technicians than the U.S. Asian universities worldwide are at the forefront of technological training, so that in a few years not only will they be manufacturing high-tech products - as they are already doing - but also designing them.

I can imagine Europeans and Americans migrating in search of an opportunity in Asia, trying to make a fortune there, a reverse trend from the past when many were looking for opportunities in Europe or the United States. A few turns in life.

Goal guru Alvin Toffler wrote: *"The educational system is a second class factory-style organisation, pumping outdated information in obsolete ways in some schools that are not connected to the children's future."*

Devastating.

11

Applied Financial Intelligence

BEFORE READING this section you should know that intelligence can be developed; it does not depend on what genes you inherit.

A person is financially intelligent because he is financially capable of making highly refined distinctions. His vocabulary includes words such as *"active"* and *"passive"*, *"capital gains"* and *"income gains,"* *"employee"* and *"employer"*, *"investment"* and *"savings"*, *"compound interest"* and *"compound inflation."* He knows the differences between them.

Dear reader, if you do not know how these concepts affect your checking account, you have three options: a) come to one of my seminars, b) buy several economics textbooks, or c) continue to lose money.

Another distinction is "optimal income" and "poor income." Are there terrible incomes? In a way, yes: poor or terrible income is that which occurs on time or only once, and optimal income is that which occurs periodically, like a flow.

Let's look at an example: do you prefer to have a million Euros once, or to cover one cent on the first day of the month, two in the second, three in the third...and then it doubles each day until the

31st day of the month? A person with no financial education would choose the first option: one figure on time. A financially savvy person would choose the second option: a growing revenue stream that would give him ... more than 21 million Euros in 31 days! If you do not believe it, do the numbers.

Another intelligent distinction is "good spending" and "bad spending." Good spending pays itself (disguised as investment expenditure). Bad spending pays someone who spends but is never recovered (waste disguised as necessary).

I encourage you to do a lot of good spending and very little of bad spending. You can get rich if you learn to spend your money well. *"Too many people spend money they have not earned, buying things they do not want, to impress people they don't like",* Will Rogers.

Amen.

"Bad spending" is the first cousin of "emotional spending." Emotional? Yes, it is the kind of spending that compensates for dissatisfaction - the automatic therapeutic gift. Do you not know cheaper therapies?

Therapy shopping can elevate one's mood momentarily, but when you get home with unnecessary purchases, you get depressed when you realise what you've done. "*Whoever buys something he does not need, sells what he needs,*" Arab proverb.

Another proverb the origin of which I don't know says that whoever buys what is not needed robs himself. If mankind can manage to eradicate the emotional spending pandemic, it would save trillions of Euros per year. If that same money were invested in the creation of small personal businesses, it would increase the wealth and overall happiness of humans.

Ask yourself these two questions to get rid of the practice of emotional spending:

1. Would spending money on this make me richer or poorer?

2. Do I really want to buy it or am I buying it just to make me feel better?

Answer these two questions before making an expenditure of any kind.

The rules are simple.

1. Never buy something worth over 100 Euros or Dollars without waiting 48 hours to think about it.
2. Never pay with a credit card or with borrowed money. Always pay cash.

I know writer Janet Attwood was being sincere when she said, "*Making money and creating wealth are skills that most people should learn. Having money and wealth requires investment of one's time and energy to learn these skills.*"

Let's learn them. I know of 12 actions that will increase (unleash) your financial IQ. Pay full attention, because you're going to learn the habits of prosperous minds.

Let's get moving on these immediate actions:

1. *Review your beliefs about money.* Write them down and with each, ask yourself if they are true or not. In my courses I always ask this question: Which ones are fresh and which ones are stale? You'll know by how you feel about each. If it makes you feel small or if you suffer, it is not true. You'll be surprised how many limitations thrive in the mind. What I learned as a coach is that we all believe in things that are simply not true - yet they seem true because we've always thought of them that way.
2. *Supplement your salary with other sources of income.* Develop, in parallel, other ways to earn a living so you earn the lifestyle you want. Start it as a hobby or passion, then you could get paid for that hobby, and then it becomes a source of income. Maybe one day, it will turn out to be the heart of

your business. I have no statistics, but I know many good businesses have started this way: little by little.
3. *Pay yourself first*. On the first of the month, what almost everyone does is to pay everyone else without paying themselves, after receiving their salary. They forget to pay themselves - they who have earned the money! But if you do not pay yourself first, is something left when all have taken their share of your pay? If you pay everyone but not yourself, then you're like working for others in addition to the company that hired you: your bank, your utilities, your government, your home ... Solution: automatically take 10% of your pay when you receive it and put it into an account that you set aside to start your own business. And then pay your bills. Always in that order.
4. *Don't get into debt recklessly*. If you already have debts, reduce your current debt - make it a priority. Shock your banker. Debt turns you into a "worker" for lenders; that is, banks or finance companies. Pay in cash, minimise the use of credit cards. Buying on credit is in fact "mortgaging" your future work. And you don't want that, right?
5. *Establish goals for growing your income every year*. For example, 10% more each year. If you are employed this may not be possible, but if you have variable income sources, you can budget the amount you want to have as income each year. Once set, you must work on the actions that will lead you to achieving it. It's like starting the income statement at the end: tell me how much you want to earn and I'll tell you what you have to sell.
6. *Create different sources of passive income*. Do not sell all your time. Invest part of it to create revenue streams that work for you. Your assets. Your income sources - in the form of property. I presume that you understand the need for various sources of income to cover contingencies, as soon as one of them dries up.
7. *Do not bury your talents in an uninteresting job*. Develop something that you feel passionate about and put your

talent at the service of others. The money will follow. Turn what you know into a business, a service, money. Imagine that you can offer something to people that will make them and yourself happy, giving you cash flow. Enough of working just for money!
8. *Train yourself financially by reading good books and articles.* Read biographies of successful people and take courses given by people who are models of financial intelligence. People who show you "how to do it" not people who explain "how it was told" or "believe what is being done." Look for real testimonies, not theory. Additionally, train in your career field as you go through the process of continuous improvement. Nothing can stop you.
9. *Do not try to solve your money problems with money alone.* Do it creatively so they don't ever become a problem again. I hope you learned that money problems are not due to a lack of money but caused by the absence of a certain mentality. Your job is to develop a prosperous mindset. As I said, money does not bring prosperity but the prosperity mentality always brings in the money.
10. *Hire a financial coach. Hire a*n expert who will ask you to do more than what you're capable of doing. This is my moment to advertise so I'll take advantage of it: I am a producer of dreams and in my classes you will learn to think without limitations. If you need to receive remote coaching, I have several online programmes (visit my coaching website).
11. *Think big.* Go to the next level. It costs the same as thinking small but it delivers very different results. Imagine your ideal life for the next three years, lay out a plan with dates, and take action without excuses. I assure you that in just three years you can achieve more than you can imagine (turn your life around). Greatness does not depend on size, it depends on a certain inner quality. No need to think of a *big business.* But keep in mind that it can become a *big business.* Do you see the difference?

12. *Start small*. Today you can create revenue streams with very little: a computer, Internet, a mobile are all you need, plus a small investment at home, and some contacts. Start your personal business in your spare time. Think big but start small.

Twelve habits that work. Don't take my word for it, experience them for yourself.

In short, the formula that has helped me most in achieving great things is somewhat vague but it's tremendously effective. It goes something like this: "Do what is necessary within the time necessary to do it."

12

Awareness and Money

THE FOLLOWING quote by Harry Palmer (author of the "Avatar" techniques for exploring consciousness) makes things sufficiently clear: "Do not apologise for being prosperous and powerful. Whoever created the belief that poverty and world service go hand in hand has cost humanity the help of some brilliant people. Prosperity and good works go together."

It's in your nature to manifest your desires. If that does not happen that means something is wrong - not in the world but in the mind - where you resist your creations. How do you know that you can fulfil your desires? It's simple: if you can imagine it, you can manifest it.

After reading this statement several times, you'll keep it forever: *"Prosperity is a state of mind."* And as such is reflected at the emotional and material levels. Reflecting on much more than a financial situation cannot be limited to a monetary balance of numbers or values. Wealth is a state of mind, yes.

We already know that our thoughts influence the material world, our body, and more. Let's shape the world with our thoughts and our thoughts will also shape our current account in the bank.

In this book, you and I will examine not all, but one of the aspects of prosperity (money). For me, prosperity includes much more than money. For example, it also means love, health, energy, relationships, humour, leisure, independence, balance, freedom, inner peace, joy, coherence, meaning, knowledge and personal satisfaction...

Economic problems are never about money, but how you relate to money, either:

- in the way you think about money
- the way you feel about money
- your habits regarding money

Thoughts, emotions and habits create prosperity, and they also create a shortage of it.

The following statement is from Joe Vitale, guru and bestselling author: *"I think our planet is what was described in an episode of the television series Star Trek, "The Permission". When Kirk and his crew land on a planet, they begin to experience strange happenings. McCoy sees a huge white rabbit. Sulu sees a former samurai who chases after him. Kirk sees a former lover and a former rival classmate. After experiencing the joys and sorrows of these strange events, the crew finally realises that they are in a planet that can read thoughts and memories. I think that Earth is this planet."* I think so too.

Proven fact: when you learn to think in terms of prosperity, the mind invariably creates wealth. I'm referring to all kinds of wealth. Because when you change the inner world, what happens is that the external world - reality - also changes.

What you do for a living matters much, regardless of the size of the salary you receive at the end of the month. No one should earn a living doing a job that has nothing to do with his sense of values. The inconsistency between what is and what is done is one of the greatest sources of unhappiness. Go every day to a place that does not speak to the heart, only because at the end of the month, there is a payment to be made - leaving much to be desired. It's sad.

Would you work in a munitions factory for a salary? Most people would not, but they would if they had to. Would you work for a company that produces a product that's harmful to health or that would damage the environment?

There are many that do one, or the other, or both at once, and employees have never questioned what they do. Would you work for a company with no social conscience? Most companies do not have one. They lack a social mission. And yet, every morning, legions of workers arrive at their jobs and invest their energies, time and talents in projects that they do not believe in ...for the sake of a salary. Is this what having a conscience means? I don't think so.

To be aware of what one is doing with his money is important. In a bank, customers ask bankers what they would receive in exchange for their money (interest rate), but they never ask what the bank does with their money. They should.

What is done with our money is essential. Would you like your money to finance the sale of weapons? Of course not, yet banks around the world invest or finance companies that, although legally constituted, engage in unethical trades involving people and the environment.

The first thing I want to make clear is that money is neither good nor bad, it all depends on what you do with it. Money has a bad reputation, but it is a neutral thing. It's like using a knife: it can be used to commit a crime, or to prepare a meal with love.

Out there, in reality, absolutely nothing has intrinsic meaning, except that which each of us gives it. It's a question of the human being who makes use of money either as a blessing or as a curse. I like to think of just and humanitarian causes that are financed by money. I always think of the more humane use of money.

The average person wants more money but deep down, he has very negative beliefs about money. For example, one can believe in the incompatibility between making money and leading a spiritual life. Some people who consider themselves spiritual speak of money as an evil but sigh when they think of it. *"Ah, if only God would give me a clear sign! And make a large deposit in my name in a Swiss bank..."* (Comment from one of the characters in a Woody Allen movie). But I do not think it's going to be done...

It makes me sad knowing people with excellent skills and do good work in the field of consciousness but they are disgusted with money. For some reason, I think they don't know about it, or hate it. In the end, they abandon their projects because of a lack of resources and instead look for and become resigned to traditional occupations.

Too bad, they have failed in their projects.

Fortunately, social entrepreneurs are coming to the scene with an impetus and a momentum: people with a business vision and at the same time committed to a good conscience and values. These people are trained in universities, have worked in multinational companies, and are now developing projects that will lead humanity to a new level of consciousness.

They work on a vision of creating and contributing to a better world. They are idealistic but have well-equipped brains, people who are spiritual and pragmatic at the same time. Some have established foundations or companies to promote various social causes.

Shari Arison is the richest woman in Israel. Her businesses include Israel's largest banks, and they control one third of the country's banking activities, as well as luxury cruise companies. But more than that, she is known for her support of peace awareness through her group, Essence of Life. It is an organisation focused on raising human consciousness for inner peace in Israel and around the world. She is also president of All One, an organisation to establish global debate on the new reality, summarised thus: "We are all connected, and we are part of One." They are non-profit organisations, of cutting edge New Age thinking, that foster individual and collective freedom for peace. Shari Arison is also involved in Good Spirit, a volunteer organisation that streamlines volunteer work and assists people who are interested in volunteering.

Companies that operate with a soul is a growing phenomenon. In Spain, for example, messaging company **MRW** is a remarkable case of social commitment and support to a long list of NGO's, in addition to supporting vulnerable groups for free. It sends everyone a limitless number of material from solidarity campaigns. Its charismatic leader, Francisco Martín Frías, asks every day: "How many people could we have helped yesterday with today's business activity?" I invite you to ask the same interesting question when you get up every morning.

Balance is the sign of identifying with the Universe. It is the result of nature's creativity. In nature there is harmony. In the mind of man, selfishness is common, and this disharmony causes the lack.

Look at nature, it offers simple lessons and delivers huge rewards to those who know how to appreciate them. Meet with nature often: gaze at the stars, stroll through the woods, listen to it talk, marvel at their colours, embrace a tree, feel the water on your skin, savour an eternal moment, breathe and take in the whole sky. All these are at your disposal.

Everything manifests energy in different vibrating levels. Thoughts also have a certain kind of energy. Our perceptions are thus our experiences. The life of every human being is the fictionalised story of his internal representations.

In short, thoughts become "things": rich thoughts, in wealth; poor thoughts, in poverty. Thus the inflow of money into your life is the "marker" which reflects how you play the money game. If you want to improve your income, you must learn to play better and develop more skills. And if you are not convinced that you're winning the money game, it's because you are losing the game. Remember that positive thinking is the origin of all wealth, material or immaterial.

Go to your favourite bookstore and grab a dozen books about the power of a positive attitude; they can make you rich and hopefully happy.

13

The Vocabulary of Wealth

WORDS DESCRIBE REALITY AND TRANSFORMATION. If you want to change your experiences, change the words you use and notice the difference. We are our words. Our vocabulary defines us. Taking possession of your life will require a powerful vocabulary, not a weak one. So choose them very carefully the way you would choose a life partner.

You become your words.

I have discovered a pattern in my courses: happy and prosperous people speak their own language, and those who aren't also speak their own language. Their language is the same but it just sounds different. Each person's manner of speaking describes in detail what he's getting from life. His words are the map that describes his life journey.

First you pronounce a word, then shortly after, the word says something about you.

Words can make you or rich or poor: they are a lever for both. I always say that words are free, they don't cost money, but they can cost you money.

Your words shape your reality: Poor thoughts, poor results. Prosperous words, prosperous results.

I would like you to understand that to make money, you don't need money, but a better vocabulary.

For example, these are very poor words: *easy, hard, luck, impossible, problem, failure, to try, afraid...*

These are very prosperous words: *mission, commitment, enthusiasm, service, opportunity, trust, investment, passion ...*

This book will teach basic vocabulary that you can use to develop your financial intelligence. It will contribute to your financial education.

Money has its own language (the way Medicine, Astronomy, Mechanics and Botany...etc have their own). That is, their own jargon. The problem is that most people do not know the language of money and hence lose the money game.

Would you be able to start your professional career in a country whose language you do not know? Of course not!

If schools teach the language of money, money problems would disappear from Earth (as what happened to smallpox in its day) and we would have more entrepreneurs enjoying financial freedom rather than employees struggling in "the race of survival." What I can suggest is that you learn about the language the way you learn any language: speaking and reading it.

The prize for winning "the race for survival" is to survive but not to live.

Passion - I love this attitude. The life of everyone is their attitude. If you want to change your life, you need to change your attitude. Add to that discipline. It has always helped me. I have concocted my unbeatable cocktail: "*passion & discipline*".

Isak Andic - Mr. Mango - is the second richest man in Spain. Together with his brother, he created the Mango fashion chain, which is present throughout the world. Only 18 years old, Isak used to fill the trunk of his car with Indian shirts and clogs and sell them in the country's markets. When he could no longer fit them in his mobile sales vehicle, he rented a small shop. Today he has the largest textile design centre in Europe with a workforce of 80% women and people from dozens of different nationalities. His secret: enthusiasm, discipline and passion.

Through words and usual expressions, I can find out what a person's unconscious beliefs are. All I need is to listen. I have come to the conclusion that one reason many people can't recover from their financial difficulties is their dull - indeed lacklustre - vocabulary.

Words, whether weak or powerful, nourish your mind. They are the greatest resource for creating your reality. Why not look at this book's cover again?

Reality is the result of a previous idea, even if it was in the mind of God in the beginning of time. This fact is verified by the axiom: if you can see it in your mind, you will be able to see it in reality.

The field of Neuroscience tells us that to create new realities, we must think "outside the box;" that is, focus on what you want to happen, in spite of what is happening at present. Someone will say that this is fleeing from reality and in some ways it may be, but it is not escaping from reality, it is more like creating a new reality.

I know that thinking is hard enough, but thinking "outside the box" is even harder because it's like "going against the tide". "Thinking outside the box" or outside of what is happening is difficult for most people, as very few are adept in the art of shaping their reality through the use of their minds. Henry Ford said "*Thinking is the hardest work there is. And so very few people achieve it.*" Yes, it's true, they sneak away from the task of thinking.

I know that financial assets shrink by several notches because people also stop growing and are not able to create the next reality they want for themselves.

When thoughts and the words that express them become progressively smaller, reality continues on its journey and also becomes smaller, a miniscule remnant.

14

30 Questions to Make You Think

THIS IS SO incredible that almost no one will believe it: the quality of the questions you formulate will determine the quality of answers you get from life.

Great questions, great experiences. Small questions, small experiences.

In this section, I will teach you the questions to ask - questions that financially clever people ask often. Think, act and talk like you are already the person you want to be, and you will be that kind of person - guaranteed.

Questions amplify your thoughts and help you think big. When you focus on really big questions, you are literally reshaping or re-designing your brain because it changes the structure of your neural circuits.

Before the questions, I'll give you 3 guidelines for success that have proven to be effective over and over again with my clients.

1. If you desire to have prosperity, you must first think and act like a prosperous person.

2. If you desire to have something different, you must first ask better quality questions.
3. If you yearn about taking your life to the next level, you must first transcend or bypass your present beliefs.

Have you ever dreamed of coming up with a question, the answer of which could change the rest of your life? That's what will happen if you continue reading and asking the 30 questions I have selected for you. Have you dreamed of having a conversation that will change everything? That's what will happen during your financial coaching sessions in our office.

If you want to take a giant step towards the life you want, you have to start asking good questions. An entrepreneur became one because at some point in his life he asked the following questions:

1. What are my beliefs about money?
2. What is it about money that seems impossible today but wouldn't be if it were to change everything?
3. What would I do with my life if I had 1 million Euros or 1 million Dollars?
4. Which of my talents can I convert into cash?
5. What specific abilities can lead me to progress in developing my career?
6. What training do I need to take a big leap in my career?
7. What is the worst and best thing that can happen if I dedicate myself to doing what I love most?
8. What abilities and talents do I have that I have not taken advantage of 100%?
9. What are my economic goals going to be in the short, medium and long term?
10. How I can increase the value of my services or products?
11. What activities can lead me to financial independence?
12. How much money would I like to save and invest in the next three, five, ten years?
13. What type of passive income can I create to free up my time?

14. What is my income goal for the next year and onwards?
15. How can I make a business run without me?
16. How can I generate additional revenue sources to attain financial freedom?
17. What customers do banks like to lend to and for what purpose?
18. How can I double my income and reduce my debt?
19. How I can protect my income from taxes?
20. If my job would disappear from the face of the earth, what other occupations would inspire me?
21. What income figure can I program in my mind now?
22. How many people before me have achieved what I want?
23. Who is my success model?
24. What is the value of what I offer?
25. What aspect must I have in my life in the next five years?
26. How I can improve my offer and offer it to more people?
27. What do I do that people would like to buy?
28. What skills do I need to develop so I can get to the next level?
29. Who can help or teach me?
30. At what age do I want to retire and with how much financially?

I can feel the echo of your answers vibrating inside me. I will be pleased to broaden your range of vision. Now you're starting to think big...

I know that from now on, you cannot underestimate the power of good questions to create new realities.

The 30 wealth creation questions that you just asked may appear to be simple questions, but don't be fooled. They are designed to produce an initial effect on your unconscious mind, and then on your financial situation. I'm sure that you will unleash the giant within you, begging to open and step in.

If I had to choose a concept that I'd like you to remember, it is this: an extraordinary person is an ordinary person who asks extraordinary questions.

15

The Change has Already Begun

IN THE PAST FEW YEARS, there have been changes in the world that perhaps went unnoticed, because of the great chaotic sea of trivial news that we face daily. They are, however, important events whose effects are showing now. Others will notice them soon with the force of an economic "tsunami." Let's look at some of the strange events that have definitely changed the world.

Back in the 1970's, Deng Xiaoping said: "To get rich is glorious". This signalled the start of China's economy racing towards "red capitalism". It was a warning that probably was not taken seriously, born of an economic giant. If we ask a Chinese citizen: Communism or capitalism? He will answer: "Who cares if the cat is white or black, as long as it catches mice." Yes, mice: money. And they are catching a lot.

In 1989, the Berlin Wall came down, and the communist system started disintegrating and disappearing from the face of the earth. In a few years communism had evaporated.

I'm not defending any economic system. The only thing I want to say is that the economic system defends the worker on the one hand,

and distributes poverty among all of them. In consideration of such a price, the communist system ensured job security, housing, health, pensions and education; today, all these safety nets have evaporated.

In the 1990-2000 decade, the world witnessed a revolution in communications and information technology: the use of PC's became widespread, the Internet entered our lives and businesses, e-mail communication brought people together, mobile phones were born, search engines on the web democratised information, social networks delivered power to communities, the explosion of software programmes increased productivity at work ...

There were so many changes that one can speak of transferring an entire generation from "analogue" to "digital".

The "PC, internet, satellite cocktail" have transformed the labour force in such a way that segments of an economic activity can be separated and then carried out in different parts of the world (outsourcing).

At the beginning of 2000 there was another strange event that changed the world. If you remember then, there was nothing but talk about the Y2K - the millennium bug. The turn of the century forced people to revise the internal dates of all major computers around the world to prevent the IT collapse.

And where was the educated and massive workforce to accomplish this mammoth task? In India. Once the Y2K scare was successfully resolved, the developed world has continued to rely on India's efficient computer scientists. To do what? To subcontract any kind of virtual work, however sophisticated it may be.

India is one huge net of all global companies that providing good quality work at low prices. This is how digital outsourcing began.

In 2001, China hoped to join the WTO (World Trade Organization). It was the opening of China. From this point on, the rules changed. It now rightfully belongs to our club. Fee trade exists between China and the rest of the world - there are no tariffs, no restrictions, no quotas, and no barriers.

In a few years, China will become the "factory of the world"; and the rest of the planet will begin relocating entire factories to that country. A country with a large population is entering its industrial era, and the other least populated countries are getting out of this era.

Let me quote Xavier Roig (from his lucid book, "A Dictatorship of Incompetence", only available in spanish): *"The concept of a job as it was understood until recently does not make any sense. And is upheld even less. We have seen in recent years that if the job held by a worker here can be done elsewhere, remotely, and at a lower price, no amount of fear or distance will prevent this job from migrating. And if the worker remains, his work conditions will resemble those of the remote worker. As a result, wages for jobs that can be done in China, but are done here, will inevitably go down."*

This applies both to manual and intellectual workers; let's not underestimate the talent of the East because China is already the first world producer of university graduates.

In 2000-2001, the dotcom bubble exploded. Financial speculators for easy money were looking for another market where they could speculate. They tapped into the brick and mortar business.

As the U.S. lowered its interest rates to 1% (dragging the rest of the world to reduce their rates as well), mortgages became ridiculously cheaper. So the banks decided to grant more mortgages to reduce their margin, home prices doubled and a new bubble began to form, this time in real estate. Real estate eventually exploded in 2007 contributing to a global crisis. Many home buyers thought they were going to become millionaires - an absurd idea no doubt. And they were in debt up to their eyeballs trying to enrich themselves but ended up poor. What ultimately happened is that when the value of their provisions in the fridge increased, the value of their homes also increased, but only for this reason.

In August 2007 the pre-crisis period started and paved the way for the crisis of 2011 and beyond - caused by a growing system of tired and old models. Family and estate indebtedness finally had gone too far. This explosion was sparked by the lack of regulation over reckless practices of the international financial system, as well as by the American fantasy that every American should own a home whether they could afford it or not.

These loans were guaranteed by federal mortgage agencies: Fannie Mae and Freddie Mac. As you see, with their very funny names and seeing the effects of their guarantees, they had no grace left. They were exporting bad mortgage debt figures to the world.

Time magazine put it very clearly: the largest U.S. export to the world in the period 2000 to 2007, was debt. Debt! And the rest of the world bought it in the form of mortgage bonds, so to speak.

Warren Buffet, a leading expert in global investments, said refinancing the debt was like "a weapon of mass destruction", as it was turning out to be. To understand it, it's like having a credit card to pay another credit card. I think someone should make this practice illegal (the sale and purchase of debt between financial institutions).

In the period 2015-2020, an enormous number of people will be leaving the labour force to retire. They are the baby boomers (the largest population boom after the Great War) - those born between 1946 and 1964. A generation that will quadruple the previous generation! In a few years, they will need a government pension, and worse: they will be withdrawing their monies from the stock market. Are governments prepared to deal with this huge social spending? And will financial markets be capable of absorbing the withdrawal of resources without necessarily seeing a huge drop in stock market prices? Answer: nobody knows, because history has never produced such circumstances.

If you have stocks or equity investments, hold on to them. Predicting a collapse of the stock market is not speculation, it happens regularly. The contrast with the previous collapses is that this time, it will affect many more investors.

The year 2000 is regarded as the turning point between the old industrial era and the new information age. The rules have changed simply because times have changed. People who play with the old rules, lose; those who play with the new well-known rules, win.

Study the following:

before:More workers than retirees

now: More retirees than workers

before:Experience is valued

now:Imagination will be valued

before:Mature age, an advantage

now:Mature age, a handicap

before:Promotion after age 50

now:Promotion until 40 years

before:Guaranteed retirement

now:Non-guaranteed retirement

before:Local markets and competition

now:Global markets and competition

before:A steady job for life

now:Many temporary jobs

before:Work security

now:Professional freedom

before:Employees

now:Free agents

before:Intelligence quotient (IQ)

now:Emotional intelligence (EI)

before:Logical mind

now:Holistic mind (full, whole, integrated)

before:Blue-collar jobs

now:White-collar jobs

before: industrial era

now: knowledge era

Do you see these changes as major setbacks? The problem is that many - in fact the majority - are managing paradigms of the industrial age in the era of information. They're playing a new game with the old rules. Guess what the outcome will be?

In the industrial era, a graduate could exercise his profession for life; today, self-training must continue for life in order for people to remain up to date. Previously, a career blossomed after 40 years of age, today a career begins to decline at that age. In the industrial age, a university degree was a guarantee of the future and a mark of economic status; in the information age a degree guarantees neither a job nor a good salary. Today, our students are afraid of not having a job when they finish their studies.

A good academic education is not enough. History proves that the phenomenon of massive employment of manpower is recent, barely a hundred years. Before the industrial age, there were more "entrepreneurs" (90%) than "employees"; while in the present, there are barely 15%-20% of entrepreneurs. Our society has forgotten the skills and mindset of the entrepreneur. You'll have to dust them off because this ratio will be reversed in the future; we will then return to an economy of entrepreneurs and small business owners and thus be able reach 90% of the active population.

If you have many years left before retirement, get used to the idea that changes and the heavyweights are looming ahead. Take a trip to the future, make a change in your lifestyle. If you want job and income guarantees, try not to spend too much time on something that can be done more quickly on a computer or that can be done more cheaply by an Asian. It is easy to remember.

There is another option, but I don't know if you'll like it: move to Asia where the industrial age is starting.

However, I have a personal fear: hundreds of millions of agricultural workers are waiting for industrial work. I was recently interviewed on a TV station and the announcer mentioned in front of the cameras that a well-known company just proposed moving his entire staff to China so they could keep their jobs. You're not reading opinions or theories, they're actually happening this very minute.

Western companies - not all - are beginning to see the light. Cutting costs a little here and there or reducing the number of workers will... not help. At the end, economic activities that employ a lot of manpower must pack up and move to emerging countries. It will not be a question of increasing profits, but a question of surviving. Make no mistake about it. It is a predictable ending, like a badly-written novel.

Early studies prove that a job for life, stability, good compensation with fringe benefits - all these have made their way to the museum of economic history.

First, we export basic jobs and then export sophisticated jobs. Jobs of all kinds (white collar and blue collar) are migrating from the continent. What is the solution? The solution would be gold collar jobs, freelancers, independent agents, business entrepreneurs with their personal business who live off their creativity and talent.

Blue collar, white collar, gold collar ... What colour dominates in your personal plan?

In 1970 (that wasn't long ago, I still remember the TV shows of the time), 108 dock workers were needed for five days to unload cargo from a ship. In the year 2000, 8 men could do the same work in one day. That represents 99% fewer resources. Perhaps these blue-collar stories do not alarm you because you're feeling safe with your white-collar occupation. But I assure you that the revolution will affect everyone, whether they're blue or white collar workers.

One last thought: how much routine is there in a job, and what job has a higher potential of being exported to let's say, Bangalore (the Silicon Valley of India)? Routine jobs will die in the West, perhaps in the world. This is good news that looks like bad news.

Before retiring, our generation will witness a work transformation that we have never known. I do not know what the future holds, what I do know is that it will not be boring for us.

In the meantime, the largest contracting companies of the future will not be the large multinational corporations or midsize companies, or banks or governments, but temporary work placement agencies.

I was recently in Brussels, the heart of Europe. While walking in the central district of Anspachlaan Boulevard, I counted over 20 temporary employment agencies in less than a hundred yards. I eventually got tired of counting.

Who are they hiring? Everyone! Workers (temporary), college graduates (temporary), middle managers (temporary), CEOs (temporary) – all the positions you normally find an organisational chart!

Don't take it out on your boss, he is so sucked in by all these changes as you are. In fact, he could be next. Temporary work has taken hold of all levels in the organisational chart! Big change is not optional, but if it is democratic it will affect all structures - horizontally and vertically. Every man for himself!

Change is neither good nor bad, it simply requires flexibility, and those who are not flexible will suffer. The world has entered a phase of exponential change and people must accept this; the solution I can think of is that we all change for the better - with the world.

Do you remember what the world was like ten years ago? If you do, it will be quicker for you, from now on, to reach the unthinkable at this time. Our parents were shocked by a few revolutionary changes in their lives; we, on the other hand, experience these every day, and we consider them normal.

Change is something of an old concept for humanity, what is new is the speed in which it occurs today. Whatever you do, change will occur. The only certainty is: "Everything passes," a Zen principle which we should keep in mind.

16

The 4 Cardinal Rules of Work

AS FAR AS money is concerned, it is good to have a compass. Without one, you could get lost. A degree of diversion may be not much, but after thousands of miles it creates a big difference in reaching your destination.

Here's an example: a plane takes off from Barcelona bound for New York. If it deviates one degree from its path, this deviation, if maintained over thousands of miles between the two cities, will make the plane complete the journey. However, it won't land in New York but near Miami.

This is what happens in many aspects of our lives. A little today, a little tomorrow, repeated over the years will lead us to the question: *"How did I end up so far from where I wanted to go?"*

In order not to get lost, let's look at the 4 cardinal rules of work:

1 NORTH: People who love their work and love their income

2 SOUTH: People who hate their work and hate their income

3 EAST: People who hate their work but love their income

4 WEST: People who love their work but hate their income

As you can see, between north and south there are two options that are accepted or considered as the lesser evil, like a consolation prize. Nothing more; or better said, they're the equivalent of despair and distress.

When I was young, I belonged to the Boy Scouts. I remember them teaching me that if I ever lose my way, I should head north. They even taught me how to spot the North Star in the sky so I could move in that direction.

I think therefore that I chose the north as the ideal professional path: make and earn what you desire.

The north is made up of people who enjoy their occupation, feel fulfilled, and are satisfied with what they do. In addition, they feel they are well paid. It is the ideal which participants are directed to during my courses.

Majority are lost in the east and west. (I was in the east and decided I did not want to spend the rest of my life pushing paper in an office). The worst thing about being there was that I grin and bore it. One can live with a bad job or a bad salary for a long time; and although it is clearly an unsatisfactory situation it isn't bad enough to make socks. Psychologists call it "quiet desperation." This steals away the best years of our life, like water going down the drain.

The south is hell. The south has something good, however: in the long run, it becomes unbearable, so you're forced to take measures because, sooner or later, it becomes insufferable.

Where are you? What about people with whom you relate? Family, friends ... the people you meet, the areas you frequently go to, and the information you absorb today will have a significant influence on where you will be in the coming years. We are the fruit of our environments. Due to the enormous influence brought about by all this, we should carefully choose what we expose ourselves to.

Too many people have not drawn a road map for their lives, do not improvise, have no browser, or have no compass. No wonder they get lost.

Conclusion: boys and girls, let's make ourselves a compass and let us follow our North Star. This book is a paper compass for people who have lost their financial "north."

17

The 3 Roles and the Corresponding Income

I PROVED to myself that it is possible to double revenues in one year using financial coaching techniques. Many people (the majority) simply cannot understand that earnings can be duplicated - it is something that is beyond their understanding. They are trapped in their limiting paradigms - their mental shackles. For them, more income means more working hours. And since it isn't possible to have unlimited hours in a day, people can't imagine having unlimited income.

Years ago I came across the works of extraordinary writer, Robert T. Kiyosaki who closed the loop. I appreciate his great work although I question his exclusive focus on the housing market.

I wrote this book to provide you with guidelines for success in any economic activity you undertake. What follows in this section is a summary of some of his teachings based on my point of view and on my particular experience as an entrepreneur.

In essence, "the 3 roles" are the three types of attitudes, values, and attitudes on how to generate income. We will look at them one by one, to identify your economic role and to help you decide what you want, on the understanding that they are not mutually exclusive, but can be reconciled.

1. *Employee or salaried*
2. *Self-employed or independent*
3. *Businessman or entrepreneur*

As you can see, each corresponds to a mentality, set of values, behaviours, and different talents. To earn income in each of these 3 roles is to make a profound change. This is why once a role is chosen, changing a it won't be easy.

Let's look at them one by one:

1) **EMPLOYEE OR SALARIED:** Having a job is a good starting point professionally, but in the long-term, it is safer to own your source of income. For various reasons, a job provides neither liberty nor financial independence. And yet, majority of people become employed in a company that buys their time in exchange for a salary. There was a time when there were secure jobs and jobs for life, things that no longer exist. Obviously, there are good paying jobs but they jobs involve limitations. What is certain is that no job can make you rich or free. I'm not saying not to love your job. I'm just saying it cannot make you rich. In all my years in banking and dealing with thousands of clients, I have never met an employee - not one - who was rich and free.

Since the employee's time is limited, the ability to increase revenue is equally limited. In spite of the fact that a lot of people want a job to make their families independent, they don't realise that they have to depend on an employer anyway. And therefore, they can't achieve freedom or solve the money game in the long term.

For someone who is attached to his job, it's difficult for him to understand that there are other possible roles that can make him free and rich. In spite of the fact that a job is a good learning place that can be enjoyed after graduating, I believe that a job must be a provisional solution until we assume another role in a few years. In a few words, having a job is good for purposes of gaining experience, establishing contacts, and getting a head start in life. But do not forget that there are much better roles.

2) SELF-EMPLOYED OR INDEPENDENT: When a person has had enough working for others, he decides to be self-employed or independent. Take the example of a technician who creates his own small business after working years in a computer manufacturing company. This role is more promising than the role of employee but make no mistake, it has its limitations as well.

Being self-employed is better than being employed, no doubt, but it's worse than being an entrepreneur. From the outset it is obvious that it satisfies one's desire for freedom. Self-employed people do not depend on anyone but themselves, yet this quest for independence may make them slaves to their own business.

Realistically, many self-employed people do not really have a business but have "work that looks like a business." What is the difference? If the self-employed drops what he's doing, his income stops. If he had a real business, that won't happen. The self-employed should be clear on the fact that being autonomous is an intermediate step, a provisional measure, to get to the third role: that of entrepreneur.

A person who is independent should work from day 1 to stop being poor; that is, he must create a system that frees him from his work in his own business. From experience, I know that many self-employed people do not create an efficient system; they are victims of overwork that make them exhausted. The biggest risk of the self-employed role is to keep thinking like an employee (doing banal tasks) and not starting to think like an entrepreneur (creating amazing projects).

The self-employed believe that they must do everything themselves because of their fear to delegate to others. After all, who can be better than them? The trouble of thinking this way is that it requires an expert in too many things and in too much time! If you try to take care of everything yourself, the results will be disastrous.

The self-employed must learn to delegate or outsource to an external team of professionals in order to get to the next level. What can be outsourced should be outsourced. The best businesses outsource almost everything: production, logistics, paper work, etc. They actually do little of the work themselves, but that's what makes the difference. Do not fool yourself into thinking that people who outsource do not save money, they are looking to gain time and quality.

3) **BUSINESSMAN OR ENTREPRENEUR**: This is the role that leads to true financial freedom. In spite of the fact that it appears very insecure and uncertain, it is the best form of security – that is, if things are done well. Now the professional is no longer dependent on others (as an employee), nor on himself (as a self-employed person) but it's the system that gives him the freedom and variable income without limits.

Before proceeding, please note that I'm not advising you to have a business just to make money. I recommend it, yes, to enjoy life, be independent, creative, and to serve others. If this does not happen I see no interest in having a business. Human beings need to understand that their primary duty is to be happy, not to make money.

I discovered that when you enjoy what you do, you earn more than when you're not enjoying. People who say, *"I will work hard at something, and when I have money I'll do what I like"* are hardly rich. Evidence exists.

On the other hand, wealth is the common denominator for those who say: *"I will do what I like from the beginning and the money will come later."* So I do not recommend going after the money. Instead seek your own satisfaction and that of others; after that, the money will flow like a river.

This means having something bigger than a business. Can you imagine it?

(Read and look upwards towards the right)

- ... A great show unfolds...yours.
- ... An astounding style develops...your professional brand.
- ... A three-ring circus performs, where your audience is consumed with excitement.
- ... Shaking your market and changing it forever.
- ... An unforgettable project - that will make you smile for days on end.

Now you now the "3 roles" and it's time to ask:

1. What is the role of family and friends?
2. What is my role?
3. What would I like to be?

When you answer these three questions you will see the power of your environment's influence. I'd like you to understand that we live in a circle of mental atmospheres that influence us. Everything affects everything.

But:

Are you playing the economic game you want to play? What is certain is that your environment influences your way of making a living now. Think about this: have you ever wondered if that's what you want? Think again.

Theodore Roosevelt caught the concept a long time ago: "*It is far better to dare to do very difficult things and win big victories even if they could fail, than to alienate mediocre spirits who do not enjoy much nor suffer much, because they live in a twilight where victories or defeats are not known.*"

This is true for you, for me, for everyone...

The first two roles are a learning place to get to the third, which in fact is the only way to financial freedom. As I said earlier, it is impossible to be free and rich doing a difficult job and being self employed. To do this, you must create a system of multiple variable incomes: assets and liabilities (they repeat themselves, something you can't do).

Realise that success in the first two roles may even be counterproductive, because the more successful an employee or self-employed becomes, the more work and less free time he has; as for the third role - entrepreneur - it is the opposite. The more successful he becomes, the more free time he has.

What we're discovering is that to change jobs is not going to change your financial condition; but changing your role will not only change your work, but also change your life!

For persons wishing to change their economic role, I always recommend that they keep their current job and start their business on a part-time basis, during their free time, and from their home, because I know it takes time to build a new source of income.

You say don't have time? I assure you that if you squeeze your schedule as much as you can, some extra hours in the day will somehow come to you. I myself took time to write four books by doing marathon days of 12 hours each day.

Each role has different values and therefore has different mentalities. For example, the employee seeks security, the self-employed person seeks independence, and the entrepreneur seeks financial freedom. And each role works to achieve different objectives. The employee seeks better jobs, the self-employed person seeks to do everything himself, and the entrepreneur looks for opportunities.

As different their values, goals and attitudes are, the skills to be developed for each role are also different. They are three different lifestyles, hence changing a role is not a change of job, it is a change in the way we live.

I want you to know that success is not guaranteed in any of the three roles, and it is certainly possible to succeed or fail in any of them. I'll say this again: it all depends on how you play the money game.

18

Working for Yourself

I'LL TALK NOW about the free agent (entrepreneur), a new role - trend - in the labour market in California, USA. As an exporter state of ideas to the world, I fear that this wave will overtake us (if it has not already done so). Millions of people choose to be agents of their professional future and to be free from the constraints of working for a company. They are the general directors of their life. There are millions of them and are increasing in number. Read on and find out what they are like and how they think.

The model was born in Hollywood and it spread into the micro business world like wildfire. They are professionals whose main asset is their talent (producers, directors, screenwriters, actors, etc...), collaborating on a specific project, a movie. When the project ends, they each go their separate ways looking for their next new project. It's possible that they collaborate again on another film because these professionals depend on: A) their extensive network of contacts, B) their creativity and C) the success of their latest work.

They depend 100% on their own accomplishments and merits, they don't hide behind organisational results that are blurred and fuzzy.

The Hollywood model is the paradigm of a free agent or entrepreneur who can fit into any economic sector.

Dear reader, I mentioned the California trend because there is a growing market for talent. It is no longer capital; talent is the most important resource. Down with capitalism and long live "talent"! It's the same for real people, who are consistent, committed, talented...and who think big.

Tom Peters, business visionary, predicted decades ago that, *"Working today depends on two things: talent and projects."* What are your talents? What are your projects?

A free agent defines his working hours (flex time), he also chooses to work where he wants (at home or at the office), chooses his customers (he decides who are worth investing his efforts on) and chooses the projects he works on (to learn from the project's challenges).

The free agent is confident that he will never return to a boring job doing traditional tasks that are predictable. He won't tolerate jobs where he's not learning much and is just sitting around, waiting for the weekend.

The era of the free agent, the entrepreneur, is a blessing as I see it. It puts an end to the life sentence of a boring job and the stupor of death of "just getting by" until who knows what.

Free? The free agent is an entrepreneur who prefers to serve multiple clients rather than a boss, a company. For this reason, he's free.

For the entrepreneur (or free agent or micro business owner or businessman...call it what you want) freedom is of paramount importance, indeed the principal consideration. He also chooses the projects he will work on. No matter the size of the projects, his intention is not to grow them, but to enjoy the use of his talents and make a good living. He want to do work that provides 100% satisfaction and freedom that are in tune with his sense of values.

Greatness is not a question of size but of meaning. This is why it is best to keep a small or moderate structure - it's the secret to survival. They don't grow it in terms of size, but in terms of freedom as professionals and as people, and also in terms of income.

Free agents support the new order. The large corporation is a model that is unsustainable and outdated. Small is beautiful!

I've transformed into a coach focused on causes with meaning and oriented to inner greatness. This is what I believe in, first and foremost.

Yes, indeed small is beautiful! The micro businesses, nano corporations, and businesses run from home are the natural evolution of the current Prussian model - impersonal and alienating with respect to one's occupation.

The free agent is an independent, autonomous entrepreneur, a freelancer who works for himself, choosing what he works on and for whom. He moves in any sector of the economy where he can perform a service and provide a product for various customers. His business is to serve. He does not pretend to serve the whole world but he chooses who he serves. The growth of his billing revenues does not come from looking for more customers, but by selecting the best clients and projects. It's like guerrilla warfare (great armies do not win wars.)

Fact: one job generates 15% more revenue if done on a freelance basis, rather than if an employee does it. Think about this: Could you turn your company employer into one of your customers?

I developed the intensive seminar, "*The Money Code: Achieve your Financial Freedom*". In one of my seminars, a participant said that working externally for his company seemed an unsure venture. Unsure? In fact, although it seems paradoxical, free agents feel more secure than working for an organisation. Many of them began working as freelancers precisely because they were fired.

Did you get fired? Engage or hire yourself first!

Most financial problems are the result of widespread beliefs...in fairy tales. In my opinion, security does not exist anywhere except as a fantastic resource in fairy tales about good and bad witch hunts. "There is no security on this earth, only opportunity." Those were the words of Douglas MacArthur.

Okay, take note: The "security" of the independent agent consists in depending on himself. I doubt he plans to fail, but rather he will do his best to take care of himself. I think the best guarantee for having regular work and income is your creativity. If you don't fail in this aspect, everything will be as smooth as silk. Your security lies in knowing that your creativity will be your livelihood, whatever the circumstances. Take these words seriously.

Perhaps the roles of employee and free agent will complement each other in the future. I'm not saying they won't. One is an employee until retirement age, supposedly at 65 years, and thereafter, "e-retired" or free agent working from home, using new technologies and the Internet to generate additional income to supplement his meagre pension.

Good luck!

19

The 9th Wonder of the World - the Notion of Passive Income

ALBERT EINSTEIN SAID "*Compound interest is the eighth wonder of the world*" due to the geometric growth that occurs when applied to a sum of money. I would like to add a new wonder of the world, the ninth: "passive income".

Let's consider the differences between the two types of income: the linear and the passive.

In the first one, the one who earns is present, in the second one, the passive income earner is absent. Can you imagine earning money while you sleep, or during the weekend, or while you're on holiday? I can hear you asking if that is possible.

The answer is yes.

Yes, yes, yes!

Instead of collecting useless things in the storage room, collect passive income for your current account.

Passiv or residual income are those that, once created (which of course will work), will reproduce regularly without you having to do almost anything. In order to understand it more easily, passive income is the kind of income that once created, will flow, and keep flowing.

Let me provide some examples and you'll understand. This book, or any of my ten books, is a source of passive income because I took the time to write them. Once they were edited, the sale of each copy generated royalties for copyright purposes without me having to do anything more except to collect the royalties. Are you capturing the essence of the concept?

Don't worry right now, I will provide additional examples. I know that it's a concept so revolutionary that the first time you hear about it, you'll find it difficult to understand how anyone can ever make money "without working."

Here's a metaphor to clarify the difference between active and passive income.

Imagine that you want to go up to the higher floor using an escalator that's going down (of course not many people do this because most buildings have two escalators – one for going up and another for going down. But I am using this example of just one escalator to illustrate my point).

So you take the down escalator. What happens? To arrive on the landing, you have to double your speed to make it. You become so tired because while you want to go up, the escalator is going down. Now imagine that you need to stop to rest. What happens? You again find yourself where you originally started - you haven't reached the top landing.

Conclusion: you can't stop climbing up, you're tired, you can't stand up... Well, that's what happens to active income earned from a job.

Let's change the scenario. Imagine that you want to go up in an escalator that's going up. What happens? To go up, you do not have to do anything, you make no effort; you stop and let the system do everything for you. That's what we recommend – because that is similar to having sources of passive income.

We're now going to look at 12 concrete examples of passive income so you understand the concept better:

1. Insurance policy commissions from a portfolio of clients earned by an insurance agent.
2. Online business for a product or service (in the section "building a website that sells" that you can develop).
3. Referral commissions from any business owned by others.
4. Online training for whatever type of knowledge.
5. Stock dividends or interest on capital invested.
6. Residual income from multi-level network marketing (in the section: "The choice of multilevel marketing" to be developed).
7. Rental income for whatever type of property.
8. Royalties from: software programmes, computer games, books, music, patents.
9. Income from licences (in the section: "invest or gamble" to be developed).
10. Commissions for financial products from a portfolio of clients in a banking agent network.
11. Affiliate marketing programmes
12. Franchise income

Again, in a multi-dimensional world, I appreciate the two dimensions that are completely different from each other: linear and residual. In the linear dimension, you receive payment for working, whereas in the residual dimension you receive income for not working.

People who have passive incomes can spend their time creating new sources of income, promote their present sources, or simply focus on living. Interesting, isn't it? It's one thing to earn with permanent and indefinite effort, the other is to receive income indefinitely for work that is timely.

The question is, what kind of passive income could you generate? Could you add a new income source each year? And if you already have some residual or passive income, what is their percentage of your total income?

Imagine that it accounts for half your income and it frees up half of your time. In the second part of the book, you will know the Codes so you can imagine them and try experimenting with them.

I assure you that creating a product, service, royalties, asset, multi-level network, customer base, a portfolio of assets, or a virtual business ...will work initially, and in some cases, will require a capital investment, but consider this: once created, it can generate infinite income revenue, whether fixed or variable. Is that something you want?

The truth is that nobody takes passive incomes into account because they don't even know they exist. Before you learned about them, has anyone ever told you about them? Surely not, as everyone's going about their way earning active income (which requires them "to be there" generating this income instead of generating passive incomes.

The raw material of life is time.

Time is your best wealth and you shouldn't sell it. You should invest it. You can save money, but you can't save time. When it passes, it's gone forever and you can't turn back the clock. You can sell your time (in fact you do when you get employed), but you cannot buy your time unless you create a system to free you from work for you to generate income.

Active income is a poor man's income. They come from a sale of time; and time is a limited resource. For this reason, limit the selling of your time (whether on an hourly, daily or monthly basis); it can't make anyone rich.

Passive incomes are the incomes of the rich. They free up your time, thus enabling you to focus on other things, like creating new sources of income or relaxing.

In short, smart people are working towards financial assets, and the rest are looking for jobs.

Financial freedom is the result of having multiple revenue streams, and some of these sources should be passive because no one can work on several "jobs" at the same time. I will never get tired insisting on the importance of generating various sources of income, some of which should be passive income. This principle is the brain - the thought centre of this book.

I am sure that you understood all these concepts, but…how does one proceed?

Well, the first is to identify and know your passion: what would you like to do - with enthusiasm - the rest of your life? Transform this passion in the service of others. Does it fill a need or does it solve a problem? The key, when it comes to money, is not to chase after it but to follow your passion and transform it into something useful. The secret is to love and enjoy what you do, offer something useful and rest assured - the money will come.

The Universe has a constitution and the first law says: serve.

Know your passion. Following it will create various sources of income around it. Ideally, create a mix of services (plural) and products (also plural) around your passion. Create sources of revenue, some of which are passive, because the day is short, and there are other more interesting things than doing business. If you use your imagination and creativity, you'll find many ways of earning money because the world has thousands of needs.

A lot of people ask me what kinds of businesses would make them financially free, and I always tell them that it's not a question of this or that business; it's a question of knowing the market they choose. Economic success does not depend so much on the means, but on knowing how to use them well. To enjoy driving it!

Sir Richard Branson, owner of Virgin, said: *"When people ask me what type of business they can run, I always tell them - whatever business you choose, do it with passion. I have realised that if things go well, the money will come. I often question myself: do I enjoy my work, does it make me happy? I believe that the answer to this is much more important than fame or fortune. If something is no longer fun to do, I ask, why? If I can't solve it, I stop doing it."*

If you spend your life in a job you hate, you don't have a brain or a leg to stand on.

Once you've created different revenue sources around your passion, look to improve what you offer (the product), and secondly, improve the way you offer it (the system). In other words, do what you do best and improve how you do it. It's called "to systematise."

When your system runs without you monitoring it, you can duplicate your business, franchise it, or even sell it.

The key lies in the word: system (my mantra). We'll go back to this concept later in the book.

Your goal, once you undertake it, is to transform your business into a perfect system in less than five years. If your business does not take off with success, prepare yourself to overcome your nerves.

When your business does not "need" you - and I hope that will be soon, you shall be free. That doesn't mean that you become a lazy person. It means you are financially free and you can do what you want: create new systems or sources of income, relax, enjoy life, or spend time with your family. In short, you don't need to worry about where the next Euro or Dollar will come from.

Do you now understand why passive incomes constitute the 9th wonder of the world?

Never before has it been possible to create new sources of income, but thanks to technology and globalisation, this is now possible. This is what is called "digital Marxism" or "capitalism for the non-capitalist". Today, there are many, many ways of making money than in the previous era. And of course there are many problems that you can help to solve.

Enjoy serving others. Transform your passion into a business and your computer into an automatic cash machine. And free yourself from the labour maze that so many people are trying to leave every single day.

20

Leverage: the Force that Moves Mountains

TRADITIONAL CHINESE WISDOM SAYS: "The wise man can move a thousand quintals with an ounce." That ounce is the knowledge that can move the world. Which is the ounce of financial knowledge that can catapult your financial situation? You are about to discover the power of leverage to increase wealth.

Archimedes said, in referring to lever power: *"Give me a fulcrum and I will move the world."* But what does Physics have to do with business? Everything. You will get more in less time, using leverage.

Imagine a world without the wheel, without the pulley, without the lever, with no engines, with no computers... Hard, no? That's a lot of work, a lot of effort. In terms of money, if you do not use leverage to make money, it can also be very difficult. Your finances require levers!

As I said, leverage means doing more with less. It means more results with less effort, less time and fewer resources. From now on, delegating your levers should be one of your priorities. Working less and getting more revenue is possible with leverage.

What does that mean? Very easy. Today, technology allows you to do more with less. Physicist George David said small efforts that create wealth are great results; poverty consists of major efforts that create small results. In other words, the rich use leverage to increase their wealth, and the poor lack leverage to get out from their poverty. What I'm trying to explain is that with the coming changes, without taking account of various levers, I can predict who will work hard and earn little money!

I'd like you to know that you have the following levers:

- Others' time - delegate tasks to them
- Other people's money - optimal debt
- Talent of others - subcontract services
- Technology and computers
- The media of communications
- The Internet
- The global economy
- Training and knowledge
- Associates and strategic collaborators

Mental leveraging:

Everyone has a powerful lever at their disposal. The mind! If you use your mind with laser-sharp focus, you will shake the world. The focused mind is the most powerful lever that has ever existed.

If you use it correctly with talent, creativity, imagination, you can create your own business without investing anything, or practically anything, except your ingenuity. Some people use their brains as leverage to counteract scarcity or shortage, others use it to achieve prosperity.

I'd like you to understand that the best leverage force lies in your mind and how you make use of it. Whatever it is you desire, you can get more than what you think. Everyone is born "potentially rich," in some way. Throughout life, however, poor mental habits cause many people to be economically impoverished because they don't use the most powerful lever in the world. Our mind is our best asset. Can anyone afford to have your greatest asset idle along? I don't think so.

Financial leveraging:

Ask yourself: How will I be able to earn income while sleeping or while on vacation? This question does not need an answer if The Money Code is learned. As you make progress reading this book, your mindset will change and you can answer it.

Later I will explain the difference between optimal and bad debt. For now, we anticipate that the optimal pay is the other and the abysmal pay is you. I'm sure you see the difference. Optimal debt is financial *leverage*.

Bad debt is a financial beating.

Leveraging time

Since your time is limited, it is essential that you make good use of it. If you also leverage other people's time, the results will be spectacular.

Turn your time into a lever: prioritise tasks, set goals and milestones, focus on what is important, eliminate the unnecessary and trivial. And then convert the time of others into a lever: delegate tasks, prepare them so they can replace you, hire experts who can do things better than you, outsource tasks that you don't want to do.

People who are employed (sell their time), and work hard for their income because they lack leverage (their effort is leveraged for their employer, not for them). Who feels ready?

In my case, for example, I have no time to train all participants desiring to attend my courses on financial freedom, so I created my audio CD ("Financial Freedom") and this book ("The Money Code") so I can reach out to more and more people and help them. Both products are a lever to reach more people with less effort and in less time; it also generates passive income while I take care of other matters.

If you don't have time leveraging, you're suffering from time delays.

Leveraging resources

Are you getting the most out of your money, your computer, your software, your talents, your abilities, your experiences? Identify all that are under-utilised and you could make a big difference in making full use of them.

Technology will help you multiply your results. Obviously, a laptop, a mobile e-mail, a PDA, Google search engine, a database manager or a voice recognition software can simplify many of your tasks. Are you using 100% of the technology at your disposal?

If you have no leverage of resources, you end up impoverished, without resources.

Leveraging knowledge

If you use what you already know and apply it to what you do, your results multiply. What I propose is to reduce the gap between what you learned and what you use. In my courses, I focus on how to apply what is learned because I know that too often people do not know what to do with the information they receive. I co-authored, along with author Lorraine C. Ladish, a book that reveals how to use self-help books ("Seven Strategies to Take Advantage of Self-help Books", Ediciones Obelisco, available only in spanish).

Why re-invent the wheel, if you can take advantage of the knowledge of others, and thus save yourself time and mistakes? And the best way to leverage the experience of others is through reading and training. Some - the majority in fact – believe that after college there is not much more to learn. And less than 5% read books like this one on self-improvement or self-help. They stop investing in themselves and consequently are devalued and impoverished.

Believe me, invest in knowledge, invest in yourself. You will create the same difference in speed between bicycling and taking the jet.

Erasmus had it right: "*When I have a little money I buy books, and if I have any left, I buy food and clothes.*" The value of information and knowledge are the number one lever in the current era of information and knowledge.

What is your lever? And your fulcrum?

21

Invest or Gamble?

INVESTING HAS A VERY bad reputation because people lack investment knowledge. It is not a matter of making decisions of heads or tails – that's gambling. Investing is getting the necessary training and information that will allow one to make decisions that are obvious, almost without risk or uncertainty.

Investing is not a risk; but if it is, it's due to a lack of financial education.

Therefore, before investing any money it's necessary to invest substantial amounts of time to find out where to invest. Investing is a work in itself, it's not making a decision. It's more about looking for something than making a decision. The decision comes after the immense work that consists of knowing the investment fund is done. And when you are well informed and trained, you can make decisions – even sing in the shower!

Allow me to make an analogy: just as in Archaeology, the tasks involve more field work; in investment, it takes more time to investigate than make a decision.

As I said, the word "investment" has a bad reputation because it is associated with risk, but losses are always the result of bets rather than investments. Investments are very safe indeed.

Many are actually gambling, believing they are investing. Don't think there are bad investments in the world, just bad investors.

A lot of people lose money in the stock market because they don't know what they are buying. Very few know what to buy because they know so little about what they're buying. And businesses are not made to sell but to buy.

Ingvar Kamprad, IKEA founder, began his multimillion dollar business by creating well-designed furniture at low prices by selling ... matches! His secret was buying large quantities at a good price and reselling at a very low price, but enough to have a margin of profit. His other secret: set aside a portion of the profits to buy more products from a different line and expand his business. Today he is the fifth richest man in the world according to Forbes magazine; IKEA furniture decorates homes around the world.

The good investor invests more time than money. The poor investor only invests money and invests very little time to find out what they are buying. I've always been struck about how quickly people put their money on something they don't know about - after they work hard earning it.

The good investor does not speculate. That means he does not buy with the intention of selling at a higher price. That's trading, not investing.

Investing is maintaining an asset because it provides regular profits as income (cash flow). What happens is that an investment turns bad when it does not provide regular cash flow, or an investment that's made on capital gains; that is, investing in the hope that over time, and with a bit of luck, the purchase will increase in value (I say that the investor makes numbers and the gambler prays).

The stock market investment is not speculation because agents look for capital gains on shares and dividends from the shares they buy.

Regular cash flow is infinitely better than capital gains. Few realise it or perhaps they do, but they either love or hate the slow speed. Perhaps most investors choose the capital gain because it is easier when the economy is growing, and very few choose cash flow because it is more complex and requires knowledge. The result, for example in the housing market is that most lose money due to the "brick" strategy.

The difference between the two strategies is that in case of a falling market, and assets depreciate, the income is still maintained. But if you live on capital gains, what do you get when values plummet? If you understand this concept, if you notice the difference, you know something that is unknown to 90% of the population.

Create assets, cash flows or income, and be financially free.

You will understand better with an example.

In the 1970s, Bill Gates bought the exclusive rights of the DOS operating system for minicomputers from its inventor. Later in 1979, he granted the "exclusive license" to IBM to piggy-back on their PC's. Then he did the same with other computer manufacturers. Notice I said "licensed" rather than "sold". If he had sold the DOS he would have obtained a large sum, of course, but that would be everything. Microsoft is not worth what it's worth, nor is Gates the richest man in the world today.

License is like "renting" your operating system to any manufacturer. The initial system DOS licenses - Windows today - represent an endless income (cash flow). Another example where the license concept applies is one of my favourite stores: Sephora. It is the largest perfumery chain in the world. Do you think that each fragrance is operated by the owner of the brand? Of course not, that store is a mine of licenses. Each brand is licensed by perfume manufacturers – the owners. When you return to a perfume store, it provides unlimited scope of the license.

What would you prefer - capital gain or capital gains or cash-flow licenses?

I will share with you the secret of investors. Good investors are more sophisticated and collect assets that put money into their pockets regularly, so they do not sell their investments. As they had a hard time finding a good investment, they also find it hard to discard it.

The world's largest investor, Warren Buffet, said: "*My preferred period for keeping a stock is forever.*" He adds: "*I like to buy businesses, I like to sell, and I hope the relationship lasts a lifetime.*"

Amen.

The simplest way is to put investment money in stocks or in mutual funds in financial institutions. They're easy to buy, easy to sell, easy to lose. Both investments are a dubious business, because when they reach the hands of the individual investor, the benefit is gone, there is not much to gain and there are hefty fees to pay.

There are certainly other more interesting investments but are not attractive to the average investor because they need to invest more time and knowledge.

The stock market is actually a betting house in temple-like atmosphere. Today there are millions of Euros or Dollars invested in shares of companies that will not exist five years. In fact, there are millions of people working in companies that will not exist in five years.

My opinion is, I don't see the stock market as an investment channel. I think of it as a gambling arena. It's like the roulette in a casino or bingo cards.

Between 2007 and 2009, the stock market lost 50%. When will it recover? Nobody knows - so even the health of the stock market must be a matter of chance. I know that the stock market experts will say I'm wrong. Maybe.

They encouraged their clients to buy stocks right before the crash of 2000 and the crash of 2008. The ones who encourage "diversification" do so because they have no idea which stock will go up. And they are the same ones who say that the bearish period is the best time to "enter". Enter where? To disaster? The stock market will crash again.

If someone wishes to try their luck at the stock market I recommend they invest an amount that they don't need in the short term, that they can afford the loss without damaging their finances.

And something else: if you buy value stocks, find stocks that yield dividends (income stream), not for their revaluation (appreciation or capital gains).

Some people seek financial advice from employees of financial institutions; what they receive are commercial proposals from marketing campaigns that are being launched at the moment. I ask myself what an employee can possibly know about businesses and investments. Think about it. Can someone really believe that taking their money to a financial institution and signing a paper will make them rich?

The benefits are not in the finished and packaged financial products placed on the display shelf of a financial institution. Savings accounts, term deposits, mutual funds, stocks, bonds … none of these are smart strategies to get rich. They merely serve as temporary shelters until a real investment opportunity comes along.

Let's be clear: Your benefits should be in your own business, not in someone else's.

The majority of financial consultants recommend investment decisions that they themselves don't follow. Only 20% of consultants apply what they preach, the other 80% do not follow their own recommendations.

Financial intermediaries, brokers, and advisers are not interested in teaching clients to invest; they want to sell financial products to increase their commissions. Millions of individuals have placed their retirement savings in the hands of financial salesmen. That is scary, isn't it?

Do you know the worst part about not knowing what to do with your money? It's this: whenever you mention it to people, a dozen of them will immediately appear and say they know exactly what to do with your money!

Other "get rich" strategies that can spell disaster are: playing the lottery, saving, working hard, waiting for a lucky break... Maybe there's nothing wrong with these strategies, but the problem is, there's nothing good about them either. The lottery is the "voluntary tax" paid by people who aren't that good in math and who do not have a realistic plan to become rich. The lottery is attractive to those who have not created their own game.

As coach Paul McKenna wrote: *"if you are going to bet on something, bet on yourself"*. Bet on your life, bet on yourself.

If you want to invest in someone else's business, that's fine, but you have to be completely familiar with them. In life, it is not about *what you invest in*, it is more about *what you know* about the investment. You can make money in the stock market, in real estate, in commodities, in precious metals ... but you can also lose money. One way or another, it will happen due to knowledge or the lack of it about those markets.

Let's talk about savings.

Let me tell you that saving is desirable, but it is not a strategy to solve a financial situation. "Living off of savings" is an obsolete recipe that no longer works. It certainly was good advice in the past. Not anymore.

How many rich people do you know who have become rich by investing in a savings account? For the previous generation, saving made sense because before the 70s, savings were not subject to high inflation rates.

Allow me to introduce a term as powerful as "compound interest" (increases savings exponentially) and "composite inflation" (reduces savings exponentially).

Today's savers are losing the money game.

When there was no global inflation, saving was a good option. However, since we started living with inflation, the money that the bank pays you is eroded because the money loses value from year to year.

I'll prove it with the "Rule of 72" which is a simple calculation to see how many years it will take for a saved amount to double. Divide 72 by the type of interest you receive. If my bank pays me 2%, then 72/2 = 36 years. Regardless of the amount I have saved, I will need 36 years to duplicate it.

Too slow.

Lets crunch more numbers: suppose you deposit a Euro or a Dollar in your bank, which will pay you 3% compounded interest annually. How much time will it take for it to become 1 million?

I did the calculation: a whopping 468 years! Too late. Not even the children of my children's children would see it happen.

I'm not telling you to not save for possible contingencies (I suggest you keep a reserve fund to cover one year's worth of expenses). Instead, what I'm saying is that a savings account as the strategy to achieve wealth is a delusion. Save up to raise the money required to invest in an asset; that is, use a savings account to raise that money - consider it a temporary destination for your money.

For those who are thinking about the housing market, I will say this: "Party's over." It's been over for a long, long, time. Those who believed that "they would get rich buying a house" by selling it for "a fortune," shall have learned a lesson by now: nobody becomes rich by buying a house.

Humans suffer periodically from "gold fever" for which there's no vaccine. After so many bubbles that burst, human greed continues to rear its ugly head.

What is left then? What should we invest in?

Let's go with what works: invest in yourself, in your own personal business.

Is there something else that you have more control over? Your job is to find "work" for your money, and since I imagine it cost you to earn it, make your money work hard for you - for your own business. Create your assets and collect them.

The rich know that their wealth does not come from a job or from a bank account (whether they be deposits, stocks, mutual funds), but from creating assets that generate unlimited cash flow.

They have a recipe: their own multiple income system.

✓ They leave speculation to speculators

✓ They leave savings to savers

✓ They leave trading to traders

✓ They leave jobs to workers

✓ They leave bets to gamblers

What the rich do is create assets that give them a cash flow - fixed or variable - and are solid over time. That's the way it has always been and will always be. The rich are rich because they choose to be rich. They have a specific plan to achieve it.

And you, do you have yours?

22

Optimal Debt and Bad Debt

AREN'T ALL DEBTS BAD? Of course not, there are debts that are very good, even great, but they are few in number. The vast majority of debts are bad. Hopefully, by reading this book, your financial IQ will improve, and I'm sure you'll see the difference in the next few minutes.

Let's start with optimal debt. Optimal debt are the payments made by your customers through your business. That is, "they pay for themselves." It's called debt investment and gives you leverage through other people's money - usually the bank. Intelligent use of this type of debt can make you rich. Debts are what make the rich even richer. You should know that the rich have as much or more debt than the poor, but their debt is optimal.

As for bad debts - these are what you pay, it's lost money. They can't be recovered so that makes them terrible debts. These debts finance pure consumerism. They are the debts of the poor. In general, they finance the lifestyles of "rich" people who actually are not rich. They do not buy wealth; they buy only the appearance or trappings of wealth.

It is the world's most expensive money because it comes from future work... and from a mountain of interest!

If you want to distinguish between bad debt and optimal debt, ask this simple question before getting into debt: Who will pay for it? If you're paying for it, forget it and don't sign. If your customers pay it through your business, smile and sign. However, learning to use debt as a lever and creating wealth are sophisticated financial skills. I recommend going without it to avoid greater evils.

The high level of indebtedness, for both states and individuals, is a symptom of financial ignorance. And what it reveals is that they buy more than they sell, and spend more than they earn. This behaviour has a foreseeable end - economic crisis and financial collapse.

What about mortgages?

I hate them. They last too long in a world of rapid change. Try to answer the big question: what is better - to rent or to buy?

From the Forrest Gump movie: "Possess nothing if you can help it. Rent even your shoes if you can".

Rent that movie tomorrow at your video store. It is very instructive.

The banks know this: they sell their offices to investors and then rent them to continue working in them. Companies know this: they sell their ships and machines to banking in leaseback transactions so they can keep using them. Professionals know this: they get their goods in financial leasing operations to use and change them when required.

And you, are you aware of these things? Still don't see the advantage?

Hint: if you own it, you have to keep it and carry it with you your whole life. If you rent it, you can replace it or get rid of it when the need arises.

Rent or buy? The decision varies country to country. In countries with a greater financial intelligence (the Anglo countries), they opt for leasing instead of purchasing. They are financially smart. They know:

1. Home ownership, when financed, is not an asset for you (it is the bank's asset because they're financing it). But for those who pay the mortgage, it is a liability. By definition, an asset puts money in your pocket, and a liability takes it away. Can you understand that getting into debt to own a home is to acquire a liability?

2. Housing, financed or not, is not an investment, at least at the time it is purchased. It could turn into an investment when you sell it (if you earn a differential). But if it is for your personal use, make no mistake, it is an expense. If one day it is sold and you make a profit, it becomes an investment. In any case, you will know when the time comes, not before.

Warren Buffet knows it. He is the world's greatest investor and second richest man in the world. Does he invest in his home? No, he invests in businesses. Despite his immense fortune, he still lives in the same house in downtown Omaha which he bought in 1958 for $31,500. He knows that a house is not the investment by whoever lives there. The great investor knows that it is an expense.

Buying a home is expensive because of the expenses that come with home ownership. A house is not an asset (it is a liability disguised as an asset). When you buy your home you lose 10% of the purchase price (factoring in the taxes and expenses related to the purchase). When you sell it, you'll pay more taxes (15% of the increased value of the property or the difference - the profit - between the buying and selling). You now see that between the buying and selling you lose 25%, a quarter of its value in taxes, which you never recover.

What's more, it is assumed that when someone is going to buy an apartment, he has some savings which he will use to make the down payment (20% of value) and to pay for the taxes (10% of value). What is better? Buying your home with a mortgage and working at a job to pay for it or, leaving your job and with the money, buying your entrance ticket and paying for the expenses (30% of home value) and then investing it in your own business and moving to a rental? The amazing thing is that almost everyone does the opposite: buy a liability and then work for a company and a bank - for life - to be able to pay for the house!

Mortgages on the average have a 30-year amortisation - some longer, some shorter. That means that during the first ten years, the interest on monthly payments is staggering: 90% is the interest charged by the bank!

Suppose you apply for a 100,000 Euro mortgage for a term of 30 years at 5%. The interest you will pay is 93,000 Euros, almost double the mortgage amount. If you increase the term and/or interest rate, it nearly triples. If you calculate the numbers, you end up paying almost three times what your home is worth!

Would you pay triple the amount of a trip or a car? I don't think so. So how is that you agree to paying triple for the biggest purchase of your life? Wow!, you're working hard for the bank.

The idea that a mortgaged house can lead to financial ruin may not fit with what you know. But this book reveals how to make money, not how to lose it. Does this mean that buying a home is a mistake? Not if you create an asset that will allow you to pay for it in cash. That is, when you've earned the money to not get into a mortgage.

Remember, first you create the flow and then treat yourself to a luxury. Always in that order, never the opposite.

Mortgaging yourself should be the extraordinary, not the ordinary.

Am I late? Have you already acquired a mortgage for 30 years? Let's see what you can do to pay it in 15 years. I imagine you want to save the enormous financial burden of a mortgage (paying 2.5 times more the value of your home), my first advice is to consult your bank about the prepayment plan you signed up for (the minimum amount to prepay, and the commissions generated by the annual maximum). Once you have that information, and realise how many hundreds of thousands of Euros you can save, you'll be motivated to take action: anticipate quotes with extra payments.

A bad adviser will tell you not to do it, because you'd lose the tax deduction for housing. That's like running a race to earn the certificate of participation rather than running to win the first medal. The tax deduction is a consolation prize when the evil has been committed. It is the lollipop that the doctor gives to the child before giving him a shot so he doesn't cry.

Tax deduction is not your goal. Your goal is to save yourself hundreds of thousands of Euros in interest, so you could retire soon and settle into a comfortable lifestyle.

I'll talk about credit cards now. They finance costs that are best paid for in cash (travel, dining, flat screen TV ...), and are not assets with a return on investment. It's actually creating bad debt. My suggestion is not to use them except for emergencies or Internet purchases. It's not a good idea either to give a credit card to your teenager. Do you think it's right to turn him into an expert spender before he learns what it means to earn it?

The smart thing is to keep just one card, with all your available balance, and cancel the other cards (annual maintenance fees are quite expensive, alas). But the worst is that the annual interest rate applied to the deferred payment is around 20%.

Now you see how an afternoon of shopping can become very expensive (you get into a revolving balance wheel that reaps interest for months, or years, after an afternoon of shopping!). I read a passage from the Scriptures: *"... the borrower is servant to the man who makes the loan."* (Proverbs 22:7).

Repeat after me: I do not want to work to enrich others. No, no, and no, nor do I wish to speak about it.

23

The Money Code

THIS IS the section you've been impatiently waiting for. I can give you the code because you've learned this far and you are ready to assimilate. I will teach you how to decipher it in a moment.

What is a code? "Code" means:

1. Systematic recompilation of various laws.

2. A book that contains the code.

3. Set of rules or precepts on any subject.

In a few seconds, The Code will reveal all the above. I managed to condense it into a simple expression that you will learn by heart.

The Money Code:
"System of Multiple, Variable and Passive Incomes"

What it implies:

- Create income sources. The more the better
- Accumulate assets that work for you
- Increase your offer by combining products and services

- Establish yourself as a very strong value supplier
- Prioritise variable incomes over fixed incomes
- Focus on sources of passive income and free up your time
- Systematise your personal business until it doesn't need you
- Sell talent relating to services or products; don't sell your time

Multiple incomes? Yes, focus on businesses that are scalable and capable of generating a variety of sources of related revenue. The more the better. I mean a "collection" of related products and services.

To multiply your income you do not need to look for a part time second job. This book seeks to liberate you, not to enslave you. With what you've read so far, you know that I'm referring to a source of passive income (or an asset that puts money in your pocket in exchange for minimum attention). Instead of focusing on a job, choose an activity you're passionate about and spread around multiple related services and products.

Passive Incomes? As you know they are the income of the rich. Once created, they continue to provide income with little effort. Since they do not require your presence, or are not high maintenance, you can have multiple sources of passive income at the same time.

Variable Incomes? Yes, fixed incomes are not essentially interesting because they have limitations. They lack the potential to grow. They lose their real value due to inflation and represent a ceiling or limit. The benefits are better than wages.

A massive value system, with products and services combined? Yes, I fully employ these concepts to explain the theme of part II of this book: transitioning from employee to entrepreneur. You can also attend my seminars and I will gladly explain it face to face.

Summarising what we have discussed so far, let's speculate for a moment:

• Imagine that you have several sources of income that will prevent you from running short of cash when one of them dries up.

• Imagine that you can "fix" your income figure next year.

• Imagine that some of your sources of income do not "need" you in order for them to continue flowing.

• Imagine that you can earn income even when you're sleeping or on vacation.

• Imagine that you own and control your sources of income.

• Imagine that part of your income flows 24 hours a day, seven days a week, 12 months of the year.

• Imagine that your potential to increase your income is unlimited.

Try to visualise it all now. Stop reading, close the book, shut your eyes. Can you see it?

This book is meant to take you from imagining it to actually experiencing it. To achieve this, I'm inviting you to read (and study) the second part.

In the first part (financial freedom), you've decoded erroneous paradigms on earning money and learned to create the mindset and attitude necessary to open yourself to prosperity. You know the basic concepts that financially intelligent people know, and you received the Code. In the second part (transitioning from employee to entrepreneur), you will develop the ability to apply the Code and thus obtain your passport to prosperity. I have summarised in these pages years of my professional experience with proven stratgies and techniques to achieve your financial freedom.

If you are interested in designing a new lifestyle, read on.

See you in part 2 !

PART II

From Employee to Entrepreneur

24

Common Excuses for Not Taking the First Step

THE NEW ECONOMY is not for large corporations, it's for entrepreneurs.

In 1900 there were 485 U.S. automakers. How many remain today? Three - and they've got problems. Chrysler has been absorbed. Two. The largest, GM, has already been taken over by the government. One and a half.

In the 1980's there were 40 computer manufacturers in the U.S. How many are left today? Four.

Dinosaurs also inhabited the planet millions of years ago. They were very large, very strong, but they all disappeared. Corporations also have surrendered their leadership, passing it on to entrepreneurs and free agents. In the U.S., entrepreneurs number less than 20%, but two thirds are millionaires.

Greatness is not about size.

Definition of free agents: people who work for themselves in micro businesses, meaningful jobs, and leading careers (general directors of their life, CEOs of freedom). They're developing an occupation with a great sense of fulfilment: pursuing a mission or purpose in life, something that's worthwhile. And not just for the money. If the activity gives meaning, the money will come.

We're witnessing the entrepreneurial revolution, an area in which women reign in their own right. Why them? Because they are extremely good at work and because they meet the number one skill to survive globally: the right brain.

I call upon all men. The left brain that generated such good results so far is not a priority in the new world. It is time to recycle yourself. Do it quickly. Women know how to improvise, undertake more, know how to relate better, and integrate emotion and intuition in their lives ... the future is theirs, no doubt about that. Men, learn from your wife, your sister, your co-workers...

Let's go back in time. The role of entrepreneur is an antiquity figure that comes from the agrarian age (dominated by farmers, merchants, craftsmen ...). People had their own livelihood.

The employee, however, is very recent. This is a concept that belongs to the industrial age. It is based on the model of massive recruitment of labour for production processes. The Western economic model has however changed, and the economic era in which we live has as well. It's already gone and taken off for memory lane (I don't think it will ever come back).

The stark truth is that in Spain, the entrepreneurial role does not have many followers. The Global Entrepreneurship Monitor (Spain, 2008) reported disappointing data: fewer and fewer young people are raised to create a business (only 7% of the workforce). The age of the Spanish entrepreneur is older (over 40 years). Many entrepreneurs become entrepreneurs because of need, not because they want to; after all, Spain is the third country in Europe, (but it's at the tail-end when it comes to creating businesses).

An economy where the highest aspirations are to work for a multinational and become an executive, accumulate years of service, promotions, and an early retirement - this way of thinking can be economically disastrous.

The question I ask myself over and over again is: why are there more employees than entrepreneurs?

I have an answer: because the education system trains students to be employed.

Universities are deserts when it comes to entrepreneurship. They do not promote entrepreneurship and selflessness - skills that have been residing in the subconscious of generations of people. In the end, it is a cultural fact.

We're told: "Find a good job." We're not told: "create a good business" (I never heard the second one, or maybe I missed class the day they said it). The financial problems of many stem from old recipes that are no longer valid. Going from employee to entrepreneur is challenging, provoking quite a few internal resistances.

But economic success is not negotiable, so excuses are not valid, only efforts are. Becoming an entrepreneur and having multiple sources of variable income does not come free. There is a price to pay.

The following is my favourite story of all stories collected in this book.

It doesn't matter that I've related this story so many times. It excites me. Here goes:

Steve Jobs - the genius of Apple - had to leave the company he created. He left a year after building the successful Mac computer! It turned out that as Apple grew, he hired a very talented person but they eventually had differences and so the Board of Directors pushed Steve away from the business.

At 30 years old, he was out of his own company. What had been the centre of his life ended suddenly. He even thought of leaving Silicon Valley, but in his heart, he knew he still loved what he did. Management rejected him, but he still felt passionate about his work. He decided to start again and he became a novice. In five years he bought Next and created Pixar, which produced the first feature length film with the use of a computer (ToyStory). It was a blockbuster!

Then one day, thanks to life's strange twists and turns, Apple was stuck and had problems. Steve bought Next and then returned to Apple, grabbing the top position of the company he had created years ago. It was suddenly worth it - what happened in the past. He was back home.

Today, Apple and Steve Jobs have become a myth. His secret: to love what you do and to never leave it. Stay "hungry" for passion.

I am writing to you, dear reader - whether young, adult, or older - if you don't feel passionate, if you're not hungry with love for what you do, then reconsider your purpose in life.

You can look for excuses and you can make money but you cannot do both. You have to choose.

Excuses, in truth, are an expression of fear. There are no advantages to fear. Fear? Yes, being afraid of putting yourself to the test, of failing, of the opinions of others, of not achieving and also achieving...

Fear has many disguises but always produces the same effect: it blocks you. It creates a very negative ripple effect in all areas of life. Stop reading for a moment and imagine life without excuses of any kind. What would your life look like then?

Tested axiom: less fear is more happiness.

And if you've ever used any of the following excuses, I hope that reading this book will encourage you to turn them off.

Consider the following list of excuses for not starting (it's not a complete list, because with each day comes a new one).

1.<u>*At my age, it is too late to have a business*</u>. It's a good excuse but I'm afraid it will not work. Today, 60 is like being 40 half a century ago. The subject of money is also a factor: if you still need money, that means you still need a source of income. No matter what the age is, what really matters is whether or not you need money to live.

2. <u>*I am too young to have a business*</u>. We have countless examples of young billionaires whose great and creative ideas have given rise to

valuable companies. For example, the owner of IKEA, Swedish Ingvar Kamprad, and the fifth richest man, started his business when he was 17 years old. Mexico's Carlos Slim, and the third richest man in the world, began at age 10 selling candy.

The list of examples is long. The amazing thing about this era of information is that never before has wealth been so accessible to young people. If you do not believe me, check out the statistics on young millionaires. They are less than 30 years old and their businesses earn millions. Do not envy them, better yet, become one of them! When you envy something about another person, you're denying it for yourself. The happier you feel because someone else has something, the more you will give it to yourself.

3. *I have no experience or knowledge*. Of course you don't have all that, no one expects you to. Besides, what good is experience in a rapidly changing world? Try imagination, that's better. In the new era, you'll always be new. It is so obvious that it's not worth over-discussing it at this point. It happens to everyone: when you start something, you are a novice.

4. *It takes a lot of money to get started*. This is the most popular excuse but also the weakest. Those who use this excuse have never created a business. They have an outdated mentality. At this time, in the West at least, wealth is correlated with creativity and talent. The rich mind is imaginative, uses the right brain, and develops your emotional intelligence quotient. Warren Buffet said that to be a good investor one must master the emotions. True. If your emotions drag you, they will also take your money.

5. *I will get training first*. I am of the opinion that the best training is to practice. It's not what you learn, but what you do with what you learn, which makes the difference. As you know, today we have so much information and training available that it's impossible to know everything. It is best to start and learn as you go along. If you expect to complete all the training available you can miss the train. Believing that things will be different when you have a degree or diploma is self-deception. Get someone to snap you out of your

trance. Things will be the same, the only thing that's different is that time has passed. I'm not saying that you don't require a minimum amount of knowledge, but never use the learning excuse to justify delayed actions.

6. *I'll wait for the opportunity*. How long are you going to wait? Look, if the opportunity does not come you can create it, invent it. It is also true that many opportunities do not come served on a silver platter but come dressed in overalls. Some don't appear as opportunities but as problems. They will, however, turn into opportunities if you polish, refine, and "distil" them.

7. *I have no time*. This is an incredible excuse - really. We all have the same hours every day! Life is fair, we all have 24 hours a day, it's up to each one of us to decide what to do with those 24 hours. If you "look" for time to develop your project, you'll find it. Maybe you should put aside those activities that do not lead anywhere. Maybe you'll have to manage your time better. You may have to alance yourself on a tightrope. But I assure you - if you do a little today, another little effort tomorrow, there will be a huge difference over the years. Discipline is the number one virtue. D-i-s-c-i-p-l-i-n-e!

8. *It is very risky*. Yes, of course it is - like everything else in life (a job is also a risk, by the way). A business is as risky as a job because there is no security. In my opinion, businesses are not the risk, the mindset is. Yet the entrepreneur's risks can be prudent or reasonable risks. When you know what you have in your hands, I assure you that risk is negligible.

9. *I need a lot of luck*. If you're starting a business, relying on luck as your greatest asset is better than not even trying. Will the commander of a Boeing 747 rely on luck to land the plane? I think not, and I don't think he wants to plant that idea in the minds of his passengers. The need for luck is a tribal superstition, an unrealistic fantasy. Do you think that they have rabbit feet hanging in the cockpits of jets...for luck?

10. *Now is not a good time*. The only good time I know is right now, for the reason that there's no other one. Saying that it's not a good time

or it's a bad time is a simple use of adjectives and is superfluous. The present moment is absolute, not relative. It is therefore not comparable to anything else because nothing else exists.

11. *I have a mortgage*. I've heard this countless times and it's the worst excuse. There is an alternative, although I know that it's not very popular: get rid of the mortgage (and property) if it's a true barrier to achieving the life you want. No material possession should separate you from the life you aspire to have. Remember that you can always get a mortgage again if you miss a mortgage payment. Anyway, I hope your project can help you pay your expenses (including payment of your mortgage or rent). If it doesn't, check it out thoroughly.

12. *I have a family to support*. Congratulations! This time I won't ask you to get rid of your family. Quite the contrary. Yes, they deserve a better financial situation and it is your responsibility to provide it. I think that having a family is the best position to take because it gives meaning to your project and is integrated into a larger context. When you expand beyond your limits, the power of the extraordinary takes over and fills you. The family is the ideal context to undertake.

13. *I need a stable income*. Keep it, you need it! You can keep it as your new revenue source grows and consolidates. It will require an effort, all right, but it is the price of your ticket to financial freedom. Albert Einstein had a part-time job at the patent office, and he needed his salary. He had a family. I don't know if he had a mortgage or not, but occasionally during the evenings, he worked on winning the Nobel Prize.

The purpose of this book is not to tell readers to get the "Entrepreneur of the Year" award; it is to encourage them to create a complementary source of additional revenue.

We're not talking about sending a man to Jupiter.

In the above list, all the obstacles I mentioned exist in the mind, not in reality. Outside there are no obstacles. We find only the reflection of mental barriers. In short: *"We don't see things as they are. We see them as we are "* (Anais Nin).

Where does one learn to be an entrepreneur? Hmmm ... let me think. In schools and universities of this country? Certainly not.

I think you need to "create" your own "business school" to practice your own business. You need a real business to learn. A real business, a real case study. You can also go through the experience of franchising and multilevel marketing companies - which are still "someone else's business" - but they transmit a lot of education as business schools.

To conclude on this issue of excuses, I'd like to quote Albert Camus: *"He who lacks courage always finds a philosophy that justifies it."* I totally agree. | If you want to justify any far-fetched theory, make a statistic, and reinforce it with an opinion, then put it before the word "principle" or "law;" this way they appear to be unchallenged truths.

I believe that humanity has already clearly shown that it is possible to justify anything if enough effort is put into it. And excuses are no different.

25

The 3 Secrets to Successful Undertakings

ENTREPRENEURS, come out of the closet! I think that everyone has within himself an entrepreneur waiting to come out. But to come out into the world, he should know the 3 secrets to successfully undertake endeavours or activities. Taking these three steps reveals to the world that the hero or heroine is inside us all.

The #1 secret to success is to change from an employee mindset to an entrepreneur mindset.

I'm not referring to only a job, but a profound change of mentality (it is not optional; it is mandatory). It is not about doing something different, it's about being someone else. This change of mentality is not negotiable.

When I worked in the bank, I met people who thought as employees while they tried to become entrepreneurs. It did not work. They were misplaced, they were in a context that required another level of thinking. They were inconsistent, and the "wear and tear" they felt made them give up at some point.

Someone who does not like his work or employment is not sufficient reason to be an entrepreneur.

Losing a job is not reason enough to become an entrepreneur. Entrepreneurship is a mindset, a vocation, a lifestyle. To become an entrepreneur is to cover a process. And in the process, the employee should die, only to be reborn as an entrepreneur.

I learned that the transition from employee to entrepreneur is more than changing jobs or workplace. It is a metamorphosis - as spectacular as that described in Kafka's novel. And you too can learn.

The 2nd secret of success is knowing what you want and be willing to pay the price for it.

Life does not reward good intentions, it rewards only efforts. Many are those who want to make money, but few are willing to pay the price. Haggling constantly, they obtain rebates and end up with unpaid balances. They want more money, but do not want to put more effort. They want a partner but do not want to compromise. They want peace of mind, but do not want to let go of their conflicts. They want to learn, but do not want to practice the lessons.

I meet people who are badly aligned with their goals: they want an effect but hate the cause. Because they are misaligned, they don't get their wishes and are surprised when I say "wanting" something is useless, because disciplined action is what matters. And then saying "*Well, I will some day*" is worthless because that day never comes.

When you know what you want, find out the price, and then pay it gladly.

I love paying. The higher the price, the better. I know that it will lead me to dream bigger dreams. In fact, I do not consider it a price but an investment. For those who haggle over the price of their dreams, they may find that the price will be higher tomorrow, which often happens.

Knowing what you want is more important than knowing how to get it. Why? Because in life there are countless ways of getting to where you want to go. The essential thing, however, is deciding where to go and not turning away from your destination.

In my courses, people complain that they don't know what to dedicate their lives to. I think everybody knows somehow what they want (your heart knows), but they say they don't. In fact what they mean is they do not know how to make it real - but that's irrelevant.

The 3rd secret of success is that undertaking a project consists of 15% aptitude and 85% attitude.

As a rule, I have always been struck about people spending much of their life by improving their aptitude or conventional training (school, college, master's, postgraduate, PhD ...) and spend nothing or almost nothing to re-shape their attitude.

This is not to say that conventional training is not important (in fact it's only 15% important when achieving the goal). Attitude (85% achievement) is much more important than training. Young people today realise that a bachelor's degree doesn't amount to much.

I have data: a college graduate earns only 43% more than a high school graduate. Too little of a difference in outcome for such an investment of time and effort. Having a career is becoming increasingly less lucrative. Once I said the same thing in a radio station, and immediately after, a young university student called to ask, "So what does one do"?

Answer:

Young lady, I encourage you to go to college of course (while a university degree or master's degree does not guarantee employment and good pay, it is far better than having none of them). But even more, I encourage you to develop a hyper-positive attitude of self-improvement and effort. There's the difference. Additionally, line up outside the mainstream education system as it is usually several steps behind reality and the market. The more vital step is that you shape your attitude - the winning attitude. You'll see that the market will not ask for school grades or college papers. It will ask for results. It values not what you've learned, but that you're learning to learn.

I've known since age seven that attitude is everything. After joining the Boy Scouts, I made a vow - "*As much as I can.*" It's been the mantra of my life - to make the most of what's in my hand every day. Whatever we do ... As much as we can!

Alvin Toffler, American futurist and author of The Wealth Revolution said, *"The illiterate of tomorrow will not be the person unable to read. The illiterate of tomorrow will be the person who has not learned to learn."* I could spend all night thinking about it and still not be able to express it so accurately.

26

Deliver significant value to massive numbers of people

THIS SECTION HAS BEEN WRITTEN to proclaim your "Independence Day" and to know the intricacies of how to earn sums of money with many zeros.

Albert Einstein said: "*Do not try to become successful, try to make yourself valuable.*" Valuable to your market. If you do that every day, all your days will be a great success, and therefore you will enjoy money and freedom.

I'll be radical: increasing your income increases the value you deliver.

Wealth depends on the value you provide to the market. Whether you're an employee or entrepreneur - this applies to is for everyone. Things will go better if you make more valuable contributions to your company or to your customers.

Zig Ziglar, a motivational legend, put it in these words: "*You can have anything you want in life if you help enough people get what they want.*" So the greater value is given, the better you will do; and your employer or your client will care little about the price you ask for.

If you simplify things that are complex for people, you'll earn a good living. Let's go, "you will make money." The rule is clear: deliver value massively. Is there anything new in it? Nothing! And it still sounds new.

The reason employees and entrepreneurs do not earn enough is they don't deliver sufficient value. Think, how can you deliver more value?

There are exceptions, of course. It could be that they deliver great value to the company and customers, but they are not fairly reciprocated. In this case they are not giving themselves enough value because they do not give themselves the opportunity to work elsewhere.

The lack of prosperity is linked to the absence of generated value. Here's an example: a commander of a commercial flight is better paid than a supermarket cashier because the perceived value they each deliver is different. In comparison, the level of expertise and preparation is so different that the value of their work is different as well.

Axiom: To be better paid, you have to be very good in your field. Keep learning, improve in your field, and increase the value of what you offer: turn your talent into a great service to the market.

Let me put it simply: if you want more you should give more (and give to more people). Thanks to globalisation, the world is your market! It is a phenomenon that has shrunk the planet several sizes, and it is still doing it.

Axiom: To be better paid, you have to serve more people. As your time and energy have limits, you must find means to "leverage", i.e., doing more with less.

If you want to earn more you must find a way to serve more people with less effort and time. The way to do it is to leverage, to "replicate yourself." How? Help yourself by having a team that can do your work for you. For example, if you're a dentist, you can hire other professionals to attend to your patients. This is how you serve more people through others. It's like "cloning you". Did you get it? By replicating yourself, you increase the number of people you serve.

Ask yourself every week: How I can my product or service serve more people?

Take the time every month to think about how you can serve ten times more people than you currently serve - either in your job or in your business. When you get it, your value - as an employee or freelancer - will have multiplied.

Ask yourself every year: What new product or service can I provide to add massive value to the market? Is it to create an offer and then look for demand, assuming it exists? This is putting the cart before the horse. Do not make that mistake. Go out there and see what problems you can solve, or how you could improve the lives of people in some way, and then make your proposal.

But there's more to ponder.

If you establish your own personal business offering a service, I suggest that in addition to that service, you offer one or several products. Complement your massive supply of service with your massive supply of a product. What product? Find a product that complements your proposal, or better yet, create your own. You have more room.

For example, take the case of a hairdresser. In addition to the hairdressing service she provides, she can obtain other revenues by offering hair care and beauty products to her customers. A yoga teacher can offer clothing and equipment and continue with the lessons. These products can be theirs, or belong to someone else. The idea is to contribute to the monthly billing amount of the business.

Think about offering a service that is worth charging and paying for.

The following words came from B. Fuller, an inventor: *"The purpose of our lives is to add value to the people of this generation and the next"*

What will be your legacy? Get paper and pencil, note down that special something for which you can be remembered, your personal contribution. Hit the fast forward button and position yourself at the end of your life, check it out...then come back to the present and write a mini autobiography outlining how the world has improved with your life. If you do not have time for both, summarise it in a beautiful epitaph. What would yours be, and how would it read?

To conclude, The Money Code implies the delivery of massive value to massive numbers of people. And it requires leveraging and replicating yourself.

27

Secret of Money: to Serve

IN THE WEST, people force their way with specialised services in a million of different innovative fields: personal coach, nutritional coach, spiritual coach, environmental consultant, telemedicine, charities researcher, personal assistant, adult entertainment, computer kangaroo, personal assistant, workout trainer, retirement consultant, biological catering ... The list keeps growing.

It's the turn of creative professions focused on serving people that contribute to a more meaningful life for others; activities that were carried out by unqualified people will easily be replaced by new technologies or by low-cost workers from emerging countries.

A significant part of the economies of Europe, U.S. and Japan, depends on the service sector. In the U.S. it represents 80% of GDP, in Europe and Japan more than 50% of GDP. But if the service sector currently employs 80% of the workforce, they will soon account for 90%. There will be more services - and I do not mean all services. I'm referring to services that are sophisticated, specialised, creative, talented, different, innovative, and customised.

If you decide to work on the intangible services economy, what services can you provide? I can think of different options within several categories, without being mutually exclusive:

• *Solve people's problems.* Whoever specialises in a world of trouble will have some sort of guaranteed success.

• *Prevent people from feeling pain.* Emotional suffering and physical pain are two marks of humanity. If your profession helps to reduce them, your life will have meaning and you'll get rewards.

• *Increase people's well-being.* To not be in a bad state is one thing, and to be good is quite another. Find ways to improve the well-being of people safely so you are well-received.

• *Make people's lives easier.* Do what you want but keep it simple. Successful businesses break down complex things into easy chunks.

• *Add value.* A good business is based on adding value in the process (if there is no value contribution, it's nothing but speculation). The more value you add, the more money you get.

• *Save time.* Time is important for your customers. If you can give them the same product or service offered by others in half the time, who will they choose?

• *Contribute sense and meaning.* Once their basic needs for survival are met, people look for meaning in their lives. Businesses that focus on the apex of Maslow's pyramid of needs will be guaranteed their future.

In a word, serve!

If you want to improve your ability to earn money, you must first develop your skills to serve your neighbour. These things are so related and are the same! The more you serve, the more you earn.

A law exists in the universe: once the cause is activated, the effect is inevitable. So money is inevitable for those who serve well.

The good question is: How I can serve more people? The bad question is: How I can make more money? At this point in the book you may have noticed that the first focuses on the cause, and the second on the wealth effect.

What comes next is always true regardless of what you do, the more people you serve and the better you serve them, the better you'll do. The more people you serve, the more money will come to you ... It is a natural and unavoidable consequence of meeting the needs of others.

Forget the money, focus on serving!

I like paradoxes because they are the beginning of the paradigm shift. Here are three paradoxes for the entrepreneur:

1. To make money, forget the money: Focus on serving.

2. To succeed, forget success: Focus on enjoyment.

3. To act, forget the result: Focus on the process.

Look around and you will find that when people focus on making money, success, and the results, the situation becomes worse. However, I do not know anyone who focuses on serving, loves and enjoys the process of what they do, and is doing badly.

28

Turn your talent into income.

IF YOU ASKED me what business you can start, I would say: translate your talents into an unforgettable offer.

Multiple talents? Yes! People complain that they have no talent. I don't believe them. Everyone has something to offer. What happens is that talent does not show up as a polished commodity, it can have a rough, very rudimentary look. We all have various undeveloped talents, and to polish them is to work on them.

The good pianist practices several hours a day, good writers write dozens of pages per month, good artists shape and mould without stopping ... I am convinced that we can all be very good at something - if we choose to.

"Your vocation lies where your talents are, and the needs of the world intersect" said Aristotle. Develop your talent and use it to serve others.

The message is: good entrepreneurs never stop improving their skills. They know that a business is never finished. They don't wait until everything is perfect to begin. They separate from the current and make it the ideal.

In business, everything is a question of talent, not money. To cite an example: Daimler bought Chrysler, the creator of the legendary Chrysler resigned (Thomas Gale). Forbes Magazine predicted: "Chrysler is dead." Years later it did die. Without talent, the firm was devalued and eventually was absorbed by Fiat.

Another example: Apple got rid of its creator. That was a regrettable mistake. Without the talent of Steve Jobs, Apple languished, eventually requiring the return of Steve's genius to steer the ship towards the success we enjoy today. Talent and leadership are the key ingredients, not money or size.

Talent lies at the heart of any business. Turn your talent into opportunity.

Identify your specific talent (particularly the one that revolves around your job or business). I call it your "star" talent. But beware, one talent may not be enough. People who are very talented at what they do could end up penniless.

Why? Because today, more than ever, we need to re-visit the Renaissance model: a bit of everything and a lot of something. Without that "a little bit of everything" things don't progress. Using one talent to nurture your financial situation is foolish. I'm not saying you need to become an expert on everything but at least you should know a little bit about many fields, and each time, ensure that you gain as much as knowledge as possible. Like Leonardo Da Vinci.

For example, my number one talent is to transmit and share knowledge (written and oral), but I wouldn't rely on that talent alone. It isn't enough. I must also continually improve office computerisation, new technologies, Internet, marketing, sales, finance, satellite knowledge.

Don't be satisfied with being good; be excellent at what you do. Excellent is better than good ("Good is the enemy of great," Jim Collins in his book: "Good to Great"). Good is not enough, or if it is, will soon not be. Be excellent, for God's sake!

Ask yourself:

1. Who are my models / benchmarks for excellence?
2. What they did to get where they are?
3. What can I learn from them?

The advantage of having a model of excellence like the shining star is that mistakes can be avoided, thus saving years of time and hard work. No need to reinvent the wheel. Learn from those who have walked the path you want to walk on, shape your success, reproduce it. Success (the art of getting what you want) and excellence can be learned and achieved by everyone. It's in our nature to be truly great. You can develop excellence as a daily habit.

J.K. Rowling, famous author of the Harry Potter series, was a schoolteacher. In the 90's she was divorced and raised her daughter on her own. Sinking in despair, she was on unemployment and could not afford heating in cold Edinburgh. She would spend her days in cafes looking for work, poring over the classifieds, and at the same time writing about a young wizard named Harry Potter. Ever since Ms. Rowling was young, she loved to invent fantastic stories; her extraordinary imagination was her talent - which up to a point had been under-utilised.

Ms. Rowling's secret? She decided to "unearth" her talent and make a living off of it. The rest is history. Today the author is one of the richest women in Britain and recognised all over the world as Harry Potter's creator.

Create your own legend. If you don't, who will do it for you?

29

The 12 Indispensable Skills Entrepreneurs

A PERSONAL BUSINESS is a reflection of its owner. If your mind is cluttered, the business will be cluttered. If the entrepreneur does not develop his talent, the business cannot demonstrate its unique talents. If the business has to go to another level, the entrepreneur must make it to that level first, before the business does.

I will share ten (and a half) steps towards becoming a successful entrepreneur. I firmly believe in them.

Football Club Barcelona coach, Pep Guardiola, used the PNL to lead his team to victory in the final championship league held in Rome in 2009. Ten minutes before leaving the playing field, the team envisioned a short presentation with images and music of great emotional impact. It was about modern "gladiators".

They won the finals. Similarly, as your money coach, I encourage you to read the following "10 essential skills of the entrepreneur" with background music. I recommend the theme from Raiders of the Lost Ark, Indiana Jones. As I write this book, this song is playing in the background - I'm not kidding. Listen to it and read about the 10 skills with intent and zeal. Feel the adrenaline!

1.*Business*. The first step is to learn how to sell. Not knowing how to sell can be costly to you and to your business. Today, more than ever, it isn't enough to be excellent professionally. Selling effectively and running a business go hand in hand. Thus, you can't be in business if you ignore or detest selling. The reason why there are more employees than entrepreneurs is that very few like to sell. Everyone is predisposed to buying, but very few are predisposed to selling.

For example, writing a book is less complex than what it appears to be, but selling is more complex than what it appears to be. Anyone can write a book but not everyone knows how to sell it.

2.*Marketing*. This is the art of creating interest in a proposal. There are better definitions but what matters is that your target audience knows you exist and that they want to be your client. The best marketing that I know is to create the conditions so that people will want to want buy from you before you even have to sell to them. It is essential that they want to meet you to buy from you, and that they know you before you have to explain to them who you are.

3. *Development of products and services*. Each year, improve your personal business. Think of new sources of income and expand your proposal. Applying yourself in effective planning means marking your goals with dates and organising yourself to accomplish them. What products or services can you offer?

Paul Zane Pilzer, economist, provides the answer: "Today, 95% of our economy produces products and services that did not exist 50 years ago, and the best opportunities for tomorrow will be in those sectors where our economy was absent." Look forward, not backwards.

4. *Optimal time management*. In fact, managing time is impossible, you have what you have, so who else should manage it but you! Get up early, enjoy the start of your day to inspire yourself. When you wake up a few hours ahead of others, you're already meditating, exercising and earning money. Avoid the temptation of doing non-productive tasks to the detriment of those tasks that are important. It's better to work a little on what matters, than working a lot on the

trivial, petty tasks. Time is your best asset, it is worth more than gold because it is scarce and it can't be retrieved once it has been spent.

5. *Ability to speak in public*. The basic premise is you should perform well before your audiences - large or small - and to know how to convey your message. Take a public speaking course or various courses. In North American universities, public speaking is given as a basic course. The world belongs to those people who dare to speak, making use of speech to influence others. Speaking in public, like everything in life, can be learned by anyone just by practising (speakers are not born, they are developed and trained!). Public speaking is a discipline that can be learned by practising.

6. *Ability for Inter-personal communications.* If you want to grow your business, you must learn to deal with people: listen to them, understand them, accept them, help them. What use is there in creating a product or service when you ignore your clients by sitting behind your desk away from people? Be whatever you want to be in what you undertake. Schools have the responsibility to develop the IQs of students, but ultimately it is the student who must learn how to develop emotional intelligence (EI).

7. *Computers and the Internet*. Personal computers arrived in the 1980s and are here to stay. Technology is one of the best levers that helps us achieve more with less effort. I imagine that you're a user already, but I want to persuade you to take one more step and become an "advanced user" of technology. Use an Internet browser with skill; using an office productivity suite (spreadsheet, word processing…) is the minimum. Hire a computer consultant who will help you get the most out of your PC. Whatever your level, I don't think I'm wrong if I say that you're only using 10% of what's potentially available. It's like driving a Ferrari without going through the first gear.

8. *Continuous self training*. In the 20th century, a degree prepared you to live and apply what you learned for the rest of your life. But in the 21st century, this isn't so. According to the OECD, today's knowledge about things will become obsolete in 5 years. The person who does not improve his abilities and upgrade his knowledge every

year will be worse off than others, and will be one year behind. A person who does not know how to "recycle" himself or upgrade his skills will be left out of the market in just a few years. Relearning is not an option, it's a vital element.

In this era, you will have to educate yourself - starting with a financial education. To do this, I recommend that you read intensively: one book a week at least. What kinds of books, you ask. I suggest non-fiction essays (95%), biographies of people who have proven their excellence (4%), and novels (fiction) with useful background information. These are reading materials that will teach you and help you improve. The illiterate today are not the ones who can't read, they are the ones who have not learned to learn (I've chopped Alvin Toffler's quotation but the message can still be understood).

9.*English*. For the time being, this is the language of business. It's the language of your clients who are outside the borders of your country. A long time ago, local markets did not care much about other languages, but today's global market uses English. Majority of web sites are in this language, as well as the books you're reading about your profession. If you want to move forward to the future, ensure that your kids learn Chinese. It will be the language of business and that of the economically powerful (by the middle of this century).

10.*A winning attitude.* It means much more than being optimistic. Optimism is a mental state, while a winning attitude is a behaviour. The optimist believes that everything will be alright, living in a world of untested or unproven beliefs. A winning attitude, in addition to projecting optimism, expresses the confidence of resolving the problems when they arise; it's living in a world of proven facts.

Confidence is optimism, optimism is taking action. I've always been confident that life - or what we call the "cosmic manager" - will do its part; and I ensure that whatever it "manages" for me corresponds to my own.

11. *Goals.* To work with objectives that are broken down into individual tasks, planning intermediate steps, and assigning dates for accomplishing them is fundamentally important. I never get tired of

repeating that a lack of goals in life is like taking off in a ship without a navigation plan, ending up lost in space. An increasing number of people, when they hit their 40s, realise that they feel lost in their lives. Statistics reveal that very few people work with goals of any kind, and this is why it doesn't surprise me that success comes infrequently to them. What do the rest do? I imagine that they get lost in space.

A Harvard University study conducted in 1953 revealed that only 3% of students had written their professional goals with a specific plan of how to achieve them. On their 20th year, this 3% had accumulated more wealth than the remaining 97% overall. Is that not the amazing result of the power that goals can have?

12. *Imagination.* The entrepreneur visualises new realities, invests a part of his time in looking at an aspect of his personal business and decides what the next level will be. He is a visionary ... of his own life. He provokes great questions - great questions that ultimately lead to new paradigms. He dreams, creates the dream, and invites others to share it. Creativity is the source of unlimited wealth and I know that it is more secure; the entrepreneur develops this ability and will never lack in anything. Guaranteed.

You can now turn off the music - the principal theme of the film, Indiana Jones. Thank you, Mr. Spielberg, for teaching us that we can be heroes of our own lives.

I assure you, however, that no one is born with any of the skills I discussed. All that we learn are developed with the infallible method of trial and error, falling and getting up when the occasion calls for it. No question here: you have something that you admit you lack and it is what you yourself refuse. Hard, yes; and true.

30

Please don't be "self-employed entrepreneur."

REPEAT this line - like a mantra - various times during the day.

Let it be very clear from the start: being an entrepreneur is one thing, being self-employed is another thing. The two are quite different. I imagine that you want to know more so let's go and focus on the first option.

Don't make the mistake of creating a "job-business" that will require more work and time from you, and will rob you of your quality of life. If you're going to be an entrepreneur, don't kill yourself working. Having a profession - an occupation - is one thing; running a business is another.

In the first years of a business, there's the effect of the owner and business mimicking each other. They appear to be the same, and in fact are the same! It is of course, natural - in principle. However, it shouldn't be that way after a few years. The business owner who remains responsible for the business does not make it grow or evolve; indeed the business lives in a sort of eternal childhood, its survival threatened.

Here is a list of warning signs that indicate that the entrepreneur is acting like a self-employed person:

- *The business number is your personal number.* If the numbers are the same, then there is no difference between the worker and the entrepreneur; a person must **own** the business **not become** the business. My reason is to convince you to differentiate the two: if you *are* the business and you might want to sell it one day, no one will buy "you." But if you own a business, you can always sell it. Suppose you have sold your business in your name, would you really like the buyer of your business to operate under your name? Of course not!
- *Clients constantly need your personal attention.* Serving your customers is always a blessing, so don't let that interfere with other tasks or with your personal life. But like everything else, it's a question of proportioning your time. Some entrepreneurs don't want their teams to deal directly with clients, they have this bizarre concept that their clients are their *property*. This is a mistake. The more your customers get used to you serving them, the more they become dependent on you. You lose your freedom! And once again, having more clients means having to work more and more. You'll come to the point that you can't do everything, you get exhausted, and you'll want to possibly give it all up.
- *Your employees need you to do everything.* If your team continually consults with you, this is a sign that you haven't trained them the way you should have. There's a huge difference between being called for sporadic consultations and making all the decisions. An independent team is capable of assuming delegated tasks that get more complex each time and accomplishes them, unaware of the absence of the owner.
- *Your income will stop coming in if you stop working.* If this happens, it's because you don't have a real business, you are

a self employed person operating what only looks like a business. Good projects will work better without the owner standing in the way. Since you will want to take a vacation or two from time to time, or take the time to create new sources of income, your priority must be to liberate your business from your direct involvement soon.

- *You possess the most talent in your business.* Imagine an exquisite apple. Do you know how many people need to consult you? Everything that is worthwhile about the business is the result of a great team. Surround yourself with your best collaborators (contractors or sub-contractors) who will let you do what you do best (and that which you can't improve).
- *If you don't have an assistant, you are the assistant.* Being an assistant to yourself is exhausting. I recommend that you read the" book by Michael Gerber (small business expert): "The E-Myth". So you'll understand why many self-employed persons who believe they have a business end up throwing in the towel when they discover that they have become slaves.
- *You're more of a technician than a manager.* If you're more of a technical thinker (doing tasks) than a manager (delegating tasks), your personal business will not progress. Maybe you like to do what you do best know (technical tasks) but don't let that ruin you. When you go from being an employee to an entrepreneur, you have to get rid of the mentality that everything will be better if you do everything yourself.
- *Without you, your business is not worth anything.* Work in such a way that your personal business creates and maintains value even without you. In the opposite sense, you "are the business." I believe that a personal business must be created with the ultimate objective that you can dissociate yourself from it. You read that correctly: *enter* into the business with the intention of *leaving* it. Not when you retire, but in a few years. This philosophy may shock the Latin American mind, but the Anglo-Saxon creates various businesses

during his life to sell them - that's an entrepreneurial trait. The next thing you should know is that the way to make more money is not to maintain a business but to sell it at the appropriate time. In this sense, your business "product" is your own business!

- *You act more like an amateur than a professional.* Being a professional should be your goal. The bad thing is when an amateur thinks he is a professional; he gives the industry a bad image. If there is something that the market can't forgive, it's amateurism. I see a contradiction in the word "amateur" (it comes from the root word "amar"). I think that the amateur does not really love what he does, because if he deeply loves what he does, he would be a professional, not a fan.

That's it.

To summarise: if you like to take action that will guarantee results, you have to be vigilant to the warning signs above. That way, you don't fall into the trap and turn your personal business into self-employment.

31

The Happy Business Curve

A BUSINESS HAS A MATURING PERIOD, but like everything, it also undergoes many changes. While it took 20 years for a business to mature during the extinct industrial era, today it can take only 10 years for it to expire or dissolve. If at this point a business is still not successful, perhaps it will never be successful. Why waste time saddling a dead horse? Applying artificial respiration is useless; if it's dead, it's dead.

The mature development of a happy business goes through these phases:

1. Start-up
2. Growth
3. Maturing
4. Saturation
5. Decline

How much time is involved between the start-up phase and the decline of the business? It depends. During the industrial era, a business - which takes 20 years to develop - can be riding the wave for another 20 years; today, the business can turn into a living fossil in five years, sometimes more, sometimes less. In some sectors, if a product survives two consecutive seasons, it can be considered as a product that will live forever, compared to others that have survived "in eternity."

But like everything, there are exceptions. For example, there are books with goodwill that classify as long-sellers, which means they sell year after year, and become part of the stock of book stores. Others are books that become fashionable and popular and sell like hotcakes but they are short-lived (best-sellers) and then are forgotten.

I always focus on writing goodwill books. I prefer running a marathon than the 100-metre dash. I think that if you're thinking of creating a personal business, it's also because you want it to be a permanent source of income, not a source of seasonal (or temporary) income.

Many businesses close shop because the owners are exhausted, working more hours than an employee, taking fewer vacations, and handling more problems. It's apparent that there are many companies that are too busy doing everything, preventing them from devoting more time to making money. They work so hard that they've barely got the time to create wealth.

Be clear about it: it's not how much or how hard you work for your personal business, it's the quality and focus of your efforts and time that determine the amount of money you're going to make.

Money is the result of doing things efficiently and adequately. And to accomplish this, there is a need to think in a certain way. As a matter of fact, money loves entrepreneurs, not chiefs or employees.

Even begging is something that can be learned. Once in India, there was a girl begging in the streets: "Give me happy money." A tourist asked her what "happy money" meant to her. She answered: "what makes me happy, give it to me, it will make me happy receiving it."

Happy money comes from a happy business that has managed to give you happiness because there is something you love more: to be free.

32

Start Small, Think Big

AFTER READING THIS SECTION, you will discover that it takes very little to start a business; however, it takes a lot of heart. In the next few minutes, you will be filled with enthusiasm in proving that you too can create your own amazing project. Trust me.

As I already said, the victory of the individual business, the micro business, the nano business (1 to 5 people), and working solo - all of them involve personal businesses whose owners outsource the maximum number of tasks. In the United States, for example, one-man companies number more than 20 million. A growing phenomenon that is also known as the Free agent nation (a phrase coined by Daniel Pink) is one that combines the advantages of working for oneself but collaborating with networks of external workers and collaborators. In these micro-businesses, the organisational charts don't go from top to bottom, but are flat and horizontal, going from side to side.

Down with pyramid organisational charts, long live horizontal collaboration networks!

Have a clear VISION (in capital letters). Jerry Engel said, *"When I arrived in Silicon Valley, I discovered a lot of small businesses that had big* plans, big thoughts like large companies do; all of them wanted to be global in character and scope even if they were just three or four people working together. The thing I found most stimulating was these companies were supported by a network of providers: lawyers, accountants, public relations people, newspaper reports, advertising agencies... In the traditional model, these providers had to be paid on the spot. Not in Silicon Valley: providers invest their work and time in the companies; meaning, they don't charge fees for work done. Building owners invest their space for a low rent amount, universities and institutions invest their technology..., in a way that gives everyone a small percentage share of these new companies and consequently, are interested in seeing them function well."* (Jerry Engel, professor and executive director of the Lester Center for Entrepreneurship and Innovation, Berkeley University, California).

Perhaps we've taken too long in thinking small instead of thinking big.

But:

Think small or think big. There is no alternative. And in the medium-term? Medium is not large, it's the next size after small! Don't let this fool you. Robert T. Kiyosaki was asked during an interview what he would recommend to an average investor, and he replied with conviction: *"That he be not average."* Mind you, not middle-of-the-road; you're either great or not great. Period.

We are waiting for that great moment to harness our inner greatness. But if you're reading this book it's because you feel that the time has come to be great for the rest of your life. If not now, then when?

Can working for our own business change us as individuals? Definitely. A business is like a mirror that shows what areas need to be improved. Therefore I always say that if you want to have the means to improve personally and professionally, create your business.

A long time ago, Goethe wrote: *"Don't dream small dreams because small dreams don't have the power to move the hearts of men."* Dream with both feet on the ground and your head in the stars, think big and start small. To achieve this, we should transform our mental, emotional and attitudinal approach in the things we like to achieve. It's not what we have, it's who we are. Wow!

Creating your own personal business from home and during your free time has many advantages (free time is not extra time, it's time you gain by not engaging in useless activities):

- You can start on a part time basis (don't risk your job)
- It requires a small investment (you can save on expenses without feeling you're investing them in your financial freedom).
- You can work from home (or better, from your cafeteria).
- You have a flexible schedule (you decide when and how much).
- Work on something that means a lot to you (a paid hobby).

You may also have some disadvantages but honestly, I can't imagine or remember any of them.

A boring job hides you behind a work station, a brilliant business will, above all, unfold into a project. Show your value, creativity, talent, audacity, professionalism, capabilities. Test your skills and create your personal business!

33

Starting on the Right Foot

HERE ARE HALF a dozen tips to start, enabling you to make a smooth and planned transition from working for others to working for yourself.

Don't leave your job. Be prudent. Start a personal business on a part-time basis. Use your free time and the weekends. My own experience tells me that it is difficult to hold "two" jobs at the same time, but you're investing in yourself and planning your financial freedom both of which require effort. Freedom carries a price that you can't negotiate or haggle over. Your motivation comes from your "hunger" for results (imagine that your present job doesn't exist and you're living off your business). "When and how will I know that I have come to this point" is a question I often hear. My usual answer: you'll know - it's when your personal business gives you the equivalent of your salary, or when you feel that your job seriously limits the growth of your own business.

Your initial capital. These days it requires very little money to start making money, if we compare it to what it was like a hundred years ago. Land was needed during the agricultural era; capital during the industrial era, and for the information era, knowledge is a necessity. Today, the raw material for money is applied knowledge.

The most admired companies were founded with very little money - less than 2,000 Euros or Dollars. Cash from their salaries. If you have saved 20,000 Euros, start with 5,000 Euros or less. This way you still have cash left to try another 4 times.

A lot of young people (like the creators of Google or YouTube) have demonstrated that a big business can be started without money, without experience, with hardly any means or resources. The costs related to making a fortune today have decreased dramatically. And yet, the excuse that's most frequently given is the lack of start-up capital. Although it may seem incredible to you, it is easier to ruin a business because of excess cash than because of a lack of it.

The problem is that a great number of entrepreneurs begin with too much cash and spend it on unnecessary campaigns or structures; that's when difficulties come about. The most common mistake when starting a business is investing the money in non-critical expenses (expensive furniture, expensive premises, expensive logos, expensive behaviours, etc) When starting a business on your own, there is one critical area: sales! Invest your initial capital in promoting your business, and use the proceeds from those initial sales to acquire assets.

Invest talent. Aside from your creativity, confidence, contacts, time, energy, knowledge, discipline, patience, imagination, passion... For those who want it most, it's something that costs less money! Investing money allows you to do anything (which you have achieved previously), but investing talent ... I assure you that there are very few who are willing to do it. That constitutes the real barrier to getting into business. Believe me, the only brake - or stoppage - is neither the market nor capital - it's YOU!

Start from your home. You can start in the room of your house or in the living room; later you'll be able to afford to have a space for your business. But, for the love of God, change your stifling grey cubicle and give it the colour of a typical chill out bar, with a bright and lively terrace, or into a comfortable armchair like Starbucks ... but please ... make do with this grey and mediocre "niche" first.

I have worked in all kinds of places and I see the big difference. When I started as a free agent, I was sometimes in a restaurant, a cafeteria or in my client's office - outside of my office. I also had two other usual places to work: a room in my house and a bank facing the sea - where I could derive inspiration. Before I set up my coaching office, I remember having had sessions with my clients in the cafeterias of the best hotels in Barcelona. They were luxurious facilities within reach of whatever.

Believe me, the majority of great companies started in a dull hang-out place. Find yours. Here are some memorable examples of companies that started in dull quarters, in a cubby hole: Disney, Hewlett-Packard, Apple, Microsoft started in a garage; The Body Shop, in a kitchen; Virgin, in a cellar; Dell Computer, in a dorm room; Ikea in a shed; Hay House, in a room in the house. And the list continues: Sony, UPS, Apple, Marriot, FedEx, Pizza Hut, Zara...

Finally, as you already see, good businesses only require these to start: a) a cubby hole or shed or hangout place, b) four copper pennies and c) tons of creativity.

Re-design your personal business. Thinking is an indispensable factor when it comes to earning money. So spend more time thinking of your business than working in it. Devote time every week to withdraw to some place to find inspiration and to think. If you say you have too much work to stop and think, I assure you that this is what's going to happen: you'll work...and work...and work. New York Mayor Guiliani led and managed the 9-11 disaster when he realised, after seeing so many people running from the scene, that someone had to stop and think. That someone was him.

Re-invest the benefits. Your personal business should be auto-financing itself. If a business depended on the money of others, it is not a business of the owner, but of others. Avoid going on credit. Businesses that start out on debt mode become very profitable for lenders, and only for lenders.

If you want to know if a business is a true business, prove that it generates cash from the cash that originally financed it. Nothing is more successful than a project that finances itself. With respect to your personal business, my advice is: start with a small amount of money and let it capitalise itself. The money of your business must come from your business, not from the bank! It is the best way to prove that your business is for real.

Six or half a dozen suggestions - there you have it, no more, no less.

Be ready.

34

Act and you'll be lucky.

I LIKE to interpret action as the "bridge" that connects two worlds: the inside world of the intention and the outside world of demonstrating this intention. The invisible and the visible. In fact, it's the same world, because the invisible one is born is taking form in the visible world.

Take significant action and you'll get significant results.

When you're a person filled with passion, you are a happy person. This happiness takes everything and fortune blesses you because your happiness creates the conscious state of "luck." Luck is a state of consciousness that you create. Say it and spend time with a person who understands this.

People have often approached me to discuss their intentions about writing a book. I must confess that what is usually brewing in my mind will make it to paper someday - when the time is right. In 99% of the people, they never write because the ideal conditions for this activity don't exist, and they put it off for "another day."

Ideas require action, not good intentions. If you want milk, for instance, you won't sit on a stool in the middle of a field hoping that a cow will come to you. Go out and meet your cow! You may have seen (and experienced) this quote from Abraham Lincoln: *"Things may come to those who wait, but only the things left by those who hustle."*

The secret is to start, good ideas are just that - good ideas, nothing more.

It's as simple as taking the first step, even if you stumble. Start somewhere. Do something now, and then, each day...

A step taken each day totals 365 steps at the end of the year, that's an entire trip. Make sure you do something each day for your personal business. Apply the "rule of five:" every day, do five things related to your goal and in time you will achieve it.

At age 16, Sir Richard Branson dropped out of school; at age 20 he founded Virgin Records and had a record store in London. In 1973, at age 23, he recorded "Tubular Bells" by Mike Oldfield and sold 5 million records. He became rich. Then the others followed: Genesis, Peter Gabriel, Simple Minds, Bryan Ferry...

He purchased a used Boeing 747 - with the right to return it - and created the Virgin Atlantic company, which became the second largest company in the UK. Today he owns more than 200 companies and employs 50,000 people globally. He's an adventurer, a philanthropist, and a great entrepreneur. His secret: he puts his favourite expression to work: "let's do it." He's what we call a "man of action."

Taking immediate action for each of my decisions works very well for me (I usually act on my decisions within 24 hours). It's an action that tells me that I have already started. From this point, the next action reveals itself. You don't have to do everything in one day, but you have to start. It is during these moments that perhaps one single decision / action will spell luck.

Do something pleasant every day, and your life will be pleasant.

As a *coach*, my advice is to reduce the lapse of time between deciding and acting. An entrepreneur is an apprentice in the art of taking action, even if he isn't totally ready. It's not a matter of doing it well at first, but to doing it first (before anything else). When an entrepreneur decides to take action, he does not wait 24 hours; this is why he is called an entrepreneur - he starts and finishes what he undertakes. He expects to make a killing. He knows very well that if he acts in the next few hours, his ideas will be brought to light.

It's the magic of starting. And luck?... Luck comes next. Act, and the more you act, the more luck you'll have.

Obstacles are not "signs from the universe" saying that you have to give up. They are a sign that you have to get off the less interesting roads, and try others. The only sign that's right in front of your nose is that you haven't tried hard enough.

Please, let's not look for any more excuses. Does a river stop flowing if it hits a stone or a mountain? Not at all, it simply makes its way around the stone or mountain. The river, by the laws of nature, flows and ends up in the sea; in the same way that it's natural for us to eventually manifest and act on our desires. And if this doesn't happen, it's because something is wrong.

I believe it is worth paying heed to the words of Ernest Holmes which he wrote in "Attract Risk and Success: *"Our thought is the seed and mind is the soil. We are always planting and harvesting. All that we need to do is to plant only that which we want to harvest. This is not difficult to understand. We can't think of poverty and at the same time demonstrate plenty."* Every bill that comes to your hands is an excellent seed for your money tree, don't let it slip from your grasp.

Thinking of seeds is an interesting concept. Incidentally, what have you planted today in your mind?

The best actions are promoting and selling. Indeed, until a sale is made, nothing has actually happened. Theory comes before a sale. So roll up your sleeves, close your first sale, and then create a business around this first sale. Find a client to start, close a deal and then develop ways of serving him and others. If it works once, repeat it, find someone else to serve. A lot of good businesses start this way: selling something they don't own. It seems like a bold move, and it is, but it works remarkably well.

I have signed and claimed advances for books I had not yet written. I also closed on an agreement to offer a seminar - that I hadn't created - for a company. There is less risk in doing business this way because you don't work and then try to sell it; it's actually the reverse: first sell then work!

Dell Computers saw it clearly from the beginning. The company decided to sell computers only on order via the Internet: get paid for it first, then supply it, assemble it, and serve it.

Ahhh! And was this to customise it to the client's wishes? No. The truth is, young Mr. Dell thought of a business idea wherein he could charge in advance so there was no risk of incurring excess inventory, obsolescence of equipment, distribution, returns, unpaid products ... quite a business genius this man is.

I'll admit, my mantra is "passion for action."

If you don't take action on your passion it's because you're not doing what you should. Period. It could be you're here, but your heart is somewhere else. And I know what I'm talking about. This conflict is due to a lack of coherence that will take its toll sooner or later. It's the perfect recipe for disaster.

I like reading the works of Mark Twain, a clever man. He said, *"if you love what you do, you will never return to work, not even a single day of your life."*

Many people - and I assure you there are many - who say: *"First I'll make some money and then later do what I love."* A few others say: *"I'll do what I love right at the start and the money will come."*

Who do you think will fare better? Mark Albion is a business observer who created the network of social conscience entrepreneurs. He cited a study made by Scrully Blotnick who followed

1,500 business science graduates who graduated in 1960. Of these graduates, 1,245 said that their priority was to earn a lot of money so they could do what they wanted later. The other 255 chose to work first in what they really enjoyed and were confident the money would come later.

In 1980, the accounts of the 1,500 graduates were reviewed: 101 billionaires were found, and surprise - only one belonged to the first group; the rest were in the second group. These numbers and percentages are rounded figures:

1° group) Work in something you love = 0,001% possibilities for making a fortune. Four in every 400,000.

2° group) Work in something IF you love it = 40% possibilities for making a fortune. Four in every 10.

Conclusion: go with your heart, do "terribly" well in what you decide. Shake and wake up your market with your creativity, and you will get noticed. Money hates passivity; but loves boldness and audacity, action and speed.

Formula One racer Mario Andretti once said that if everything seems under control, it's because you're not going fast enough. Start running and run fast (at the end of the book I will relate to you an extraordinary story which I hope will increase your speed, even your altitude).

Some people think that to achieve extraordinary results, they must be "extraordinary persons"; like they don't consider themselves as such, so don't even begin. I would like you to read this twice: the trick is to be an ordinary person doing extraordinary things. It's not so much about you, but more about what you experience or go through when you undertake creative action. I always say that the Universe looks for volunteers who are willing to create.

Are you ready? Get set, go!

Note: It's wonderful to read an inspiring book and to understand a new idea, understand the theory...but it's frightening to have this information and not apply and practice it. I've just defined the folly and foolishness: having knowledge and deciding to ignore it or not use it.

What if you take this section super seriously?

35

The Keys to Undertaking and Starting

IMAGINE that you're in my coaching office in Barcelona discussing about how to make your financial situation grow. Come...come into my office and settle comfortably in this Zen-like atmosphere.

The first thing I ask you is: What do you want to achieve or like to improve in your life? In a few minutes we will create a climate of collaboration and trust. Then we will review your values and talents, what you do well, and what you can do better. We will imagine that you will change your life when you have achieved your financial freedom and we will set your goals.

In our revealing and enlightening conversation, I will ask you more questions, and you will ask me as well; but I'm sure you'll want to know what helped me become an info-preneur. I will share with you some of the things I learned from my experience.

I could write a whole book on what I now know about the entrepreneurial profession, but I'm going to summarise it, in a few paragraphs, so that you leave my coaching office significantly more confident, and with the certainty that something good will happen. That's the advice I give to those who start a personal business.

I confess that the turning point in my career came about when I discovered the importance of the following rules:

Combine products and services - If yours is a product, you need to complement it with a service, and vice-versa. Using only one of these two sources of income is a huge mistake. Here's a practical example: if you sell air conditioners, you must also sell maintenance and installation services. If you sell training, package it into different products: CD, DVD, Manual...and sell it. The banks call it "cross-selling."

Banks believe it is more acceptable for a client to sell more than one product. Let's say that three and five different products to sell to clients is a healthy symptom of the business strength of his sales network. Services are very gratifying because they facilitate direct contact with the client, but they are inconvenient in terms of demanding your time. A product is more rewarding because you can deliver it without spending too much time. The ideal is a cross-sell, a combination of your products and services.

Communicate your offer - Sales are the result of a structured conversation. If you are capable of converting your conversations into orders, you're a real business person. In sales, what counts is not who you know, but who know you. If your sales strategy is to know more people in order to sell to them, you will become exhausted because being close to so many people requires energy and time.

But if your sales strategy is for people to know you, they will be the ones to approach you to buy from you. You ask, "how can we make clients approach us?"

I thought you weren't going to ask me.

Simple: use the Internet, get references, work with a smart marketing approach, position yourself in your market, become an expert or authority in your field. In short, you're doing it such that clients can find you... And this I believe is enough to start.

Choose your ideal clients -You cannot offer something useful to everyone, so you should choose your clients. I don't think that anyone should be your client. Think about it, if everyone was your client, no one is really your client.

Rule out the people you don't like to sell to and dedicate your time to those you want to sell to. Work only with clients who inspire you and whom you inspire.

Author David Maister said it clearly: *"Why spend the best part of this life working for acceptable clients in things that are merely tolerable when, with a bit of effort into customer relations, marketing, and sales, you can spend your days working with interesting people on exciting things."*

To be able to choose the right clients, you need to answer these questions: Who is my ideal client? And, who would I like to deal with in my profession? Clients who are "cool", no doubt. Why? Because you are your clients.

What's your ideal client like? He has three characteristics:

1. He asks you for more services or more products because they're valuable to him.
2. He brings out the best in you as a professional.
3. He refers other people to you.

You will recognise the ideal client because you enjoy him and he gives you a lot of energy; he doesn't drain you of energy. But if you work with clients who don't have any "chemistry", the relationship will be frustrating for both of you.

For example, my ideal client is a woman of any age, loves to read, invests in herself, is financially independent, prioritises her personal development, lives conscientiously and spiritually, values my work, and recommends me to her friends... More or less.

Now you have 3 good questions to answer (stop your reading and note down your answers).

- First: Who is your ideal client?

- Second: What does your ideal client want?
- Third: How do you serve your ideal client?

Get excited about your personal business - Don't get involved in something that you don't really love, it won't work. And you should do it now, don't wait until everything is going well. Things will never go well if you don't make space for excellence (projects, clients, collaborators, ideas...) There's a Romanian proverb that says, *better a mouse in the pot than no meat at all.* Which means, better not be in the wrong pot, otherwise you risk indigestion.

Abandon what's regular and even what's good so you can focus exclusively on what's astounding. Don't lower the bar. There's a reason: you are what you do (you transform into it) I've come across statistics that confirm that only 20% of people who work love what they do. And 80% get up every day for nothing else but for a salary. I can't stop thinking about it and wondering how the world would be if this proportion was reversed.

Design - Although yours is a service (and not a product) you have to design it anyway. Design applies (or must apply) to all businesses. All of us "design" in our profession: the clothes we wear, the vocabulary we use, the arguments we advance, our promotional material, our offices...

So you have to "design" yourself to get into serious business. Philippe Starck (if you don't know him, look in Wikipedia and grab some of his designs at once). He is highly regarded in the world of design.

Let's now go to Japan. The president of Sony said: *"At Sony, we assume that all products of our competitors basically have the same technology. What distinguishes our products is design."*

You see why design is essential?

Define your price policy - In your market, you there is always someone who is ready to compete with a lower price. This situation echoes a war situation - everyone loses. The recipe for disaster is a price policy that will make you # 1 ... in low prices.

Many, and I say many, businesses have closed because they were engaged in absurd price competitions. Let others sell on price. Price is not what makes you stand out. If you're going to compete on price, it is better to compete in the high-end price range. At least this kind of price war does not undermine the contenders.

Yes, position yourself in the high end of the price range where you can compete in prestige. The intermediate price range wouldn't be interesting because it's an invisible zone, as far as the eyes of the market are concerned (it's also where's there's a greater concentration of competitors).

Differentiate yourself - Your differentiated offer will give you visibility. To be "visible" in business is everything. Too many projects close due to an excess number of *possible clients*, and a shortage of *real clients*. I remember the change experienced by a client when he realised his problem was that he was "invisible" (he could not differentiate his product or himself to anyone, he was running his business out of sheer mimicry).

Continuous improvement - I have a two-word formula for financial success: continuous improvement. I suggest continuous improvement (Kaizen) both for you and your business. Develop your offer, year after year, until you transform your offer into something brilliant. Your clients will appreciate it and respond to your offer enthusiastically.

Life is a series of continuous improvements. Businesses are no exception to this rule. Sell, improve; sell, improve; sell, improve... Bring out the professional in you and show yourself to the world. Change your 1.0 version, upgrade to 2.0 and so on...If you invest 3% of your annual income to training, you will advance. Think of this question frequently: "Why should a client choose me instead of someone else"?

I could mention additional key tips, but let's not dwell on them, instead let's leave them for our *online* coaching session, via Skype or in person. I guarantee that if you just take and practice half of what I said earlier, your personal business will shine.

I can almost see it.

36

Your Business Needs a Super and Irresistible Product

I WILL SHARE with you one of my best performing strategies as an entrepreneur: I create and sell my own products. A product is a source of additional revenue for your system of multiple and passive incomes. If you don't have your own products, you can sell the products of others. Needless to say, if you choose to sell the products of others, you have to believe in these products 100%.

What products can you offer to your market? I can think of several product categories, without limiting ourselves exclusively to these:

✓ Products that satisfy our main needs

✓ Products that satisfy our secondary needs

✓ Products that are new, innovative, and original

✓ Old products that have been redesigned or improvised upon

✓ Products that have been improved from previous versions

✓ Products that are customised / personalised for the customer

✓ Seasonal products

Your personal business needs a flagship product that will please many people. It's your super product: the star of the show in your three-ring circus.

Offer the right product at the right time and for the right target audience (the right synchronisation of your efforts). To do this, you will have to fill a need before anyone else does, provide it better than anyone, or provide it differently from others. Of course, it will be imitated, but while others are striving to imitate you, you are already developing your product's next evolution: 2.0, 3.0 ...

When I worked for Bankinter, the industry's most innovative bank, I was surprised that executive management was not bothered at all by other banks imitating it. Instead, they considered it a compliment and lived with it. The bank always managed to be a step ahead in innovation, while others were simply "tailgating."

As far as the competition was concerned, imitating us was actually a disadvantage for them because when they joined the trend, it was already very mature or depleted; they arrived late.

As an author, I realise that others in the industry are imitating me. Am I bothered by it? No. When the market looks at proposals from my imitators, they hear an echo of my voice - in a sense. How's that for free advertising?

Don't worry about the competition. It's a good sign. At least it means there is a market. What is unusual is to not have any competition, that means there is no market. So get out of that "business" quickly! And don't keep an eye on what the competition is doing. Look at your own product or service, otherwise you could be changing direction.

You want some ideas to start your own business. I will say that the best you can do is to ask your heart what will make you happy. In the meantime, as you wait for answers from your heart, here's a list of activities or low cost businesses that can be good sources of income for you:

Catering service, being a home chef, cooking instructor, designing newsletters, editing, being a virtual assistant, personal assistant, translator, picking up kids, being a children's coach, info-preneur, designing websites, selling on eBay, trading online, personal coaching, offering doula services, teaching and lecturing, being an image consultant, manager, pet trainer, dog walker, personal shopper, garden and landscape designer, therapist, power point presentations designer, graphic designer, event organizer, theme blog advertising, children's party planner, outlets, renting the apartment as an office during working hours, joining affiliate programs on the Internet, being a "quality rater" for Google, mentoring, consulting, freelance writing, writing assistant for content...

Odd jobs? Perhaps, but I assure you that someday, only odd jobs will exist so find your rarity soon. For example, a woman named Debra Fine invented her current profession (small talk consultant). She realised that some people were unable to start a conversation and break the ice. Since she is a very outgoing person, she applied her talent to fill that need. I do not know if it is "work" or not; what's important is she has customers and makes money doing what she enjoys.

When someone says "*I do not know what to pursue*", I can hardly believe it. There are so many things to do in this world! And the list keeps growing. As an expert said: *"Many of my best ideas to start new businesses come from starting conversations with people, or when I hear something in passing. The true entrepreneur never has his antennas on off mode."* (words of Richard Branson).

Products are classified into four main categories:

1)"Unknown" products: No one knows for sure how successful new products will be. At the early stages, all products are not known; the only way to find out is to test them, or to take them to the market.

2)"Star" products: If your product has already reached a good position in the market because of its growth, it is a "star" product. However, a star product doesn't necessarily create benefits and the challenge is to convert it into a "cow" product.

3) "Cow" products. When the personal business has achieved a competitive position in its market, is generating income, and the entrepreneur is reaping the benefits ("milking the cow") - the product is called a "cow" product.

4) "Dog" Products: If the product has a slow growth, it is a "dog" product (no offense meant). Because of its slow growth, the product consumes resources that could be spent on other faster developing products. It's time to consider whether to continue with it or replace it.

Do you have more dogs than cows? More unknowns than stars?

The important thing is know when to enter and when to exit a business. The average person gets into trends that can be exhausting and then decides it's time to leave the business. This lack of vision can be catastrophic: quite frankly, I am aware that some people start a business that is no longer a business.

When is the time to do something different? When all goes well; the reason being that when things go wrong, it's difficult for anyone to think or concentrate on anything.

Let's pay heed to the words of Sir Richard Branson, CEO of Virgin Group: *"Any new product or service offered by the Virgin group must (1) be of the highest quality, (2) provide a valuable service, (3) be innovative, (4) radically challenge existing alternatives, and (5) provide entertainment."*

In short, if you blindly believe in a super product, promote it and turn it into a dairy cow.

37

Use a Proven Success Model

IT HAS BEEN PROVEN that having good references for your success is everything. If you can identify people or businesses you admire, you will learn to model your own success. Learn from those who know, not those who do not know. Use those models as road maps. Providing benchmarks for success can give you a quantum leap as you transition from being an employee to becoming an entrepreneur, saving you time and making you avoid mistakes.

Modelling is a process of accelerated learning. It is the fastest way to get what you want. Do not fret with the idea of "But I want to be myself". No doubt you do, do it your way of course, but get some help. A reference gives you the confidence to know what others - before you - have accomplished. If thousands, or hundreds of thousands got what they want, why shouldn't you get it as well?

Examine foreign markets where you will find hundreds of products and services waiting to enter your market. Find your opportunity. Become a distributor, join a network, and take advantage of the new global economy. Introduce a great product to your market through your personal business.

Where is your opportunity? Have you ever used services or products that you liked a lot? There's your chance. The product worked with you, why not want other people to enjoy it? Place your bet on what you believe in as a user of that product or service. Adapt it, redesign it, personalise, and distribute it ... but do something that adds value.

In short, your big break as a "leader" may include:

- Symphony I: Adapting an idea that works in other countries
- Symphony II: Identifying an unsatisfied need
- Symphony III: Improving a product or service that already exists
- Symphony IV: Promoting something that improves the lives of people in some aspect

Do you see the opportunities? Do you hear how each song sounds? Can you imagine directing it?

Proven fact: success follows models, references, protocols, recipes, laws. Everything about success is written, so achieving it is a matter of learning the rules and repeating them.

Money also has its own code. It is not a secret, although it is hardly ever applied. People are surprised when I explain that expressing a wish is as simple as applying the recipe for a pasta dish. It's so simple and so routine that it makes anyone yawn.

In my lectures on business, I give guidelines like the ones from this incomplete list and also share the common mistakes made by entrepreneurs. Unfortunately, too many entrepreneurs seem bent on ending their businesses. Failure is not an accident or a coincidence; it is the sum of uncorrected errors.

Let's say you want to design websites. You have an idea and you start your business, plunging head on into your project. As you go about setting up your business, be sure you don't meet with these same stumbling blocks:

Stumbling block # 1: Not differentiating yourself. In our example, web design is too generic. You have to differentiate, find your niche market to become a specialist. You can, for example, design websites for online stores. Many entrepreneurs believe that they should serve everyone and see specialisation as a limiting factor for their business. Quite the opposite. If you want to serve everyone, you end up not serving anyone. It begins in a very specific segment; from there, expand your offer.

Stumbling block # 2: Not having an action plan. If you don't have a plan you can end up ...anywhere. It's like getting lost in space! Without a business plan you have no idea. And without ideas that materialise, there is no money to be made - like dreams that are forgotten upon waking. You need to create a vision, to formulate a mission on the values of your project, and then create your business model. Without that, your offer is blurred, vague. For example, our web designer in the example I used will not attract investors if he doesn't have a convincing business model.

Stumbling block # 3: Printing a ton of brochures before starting. You cannot imagine how many times you will change your business model on the fly (as you slowly discover what works and what does not). So what will you do with that expensive box of brochures that you no longer need? When you've been working for six months on it, you will be a little clearer about your business model. Only at that time will you order your advertising material, brochures, business cards, logo, etc...

Stumbling block # 4: Explaining what you do and how you do it. It's irrelevant. It's more effective to explain the benefits and advantages for your customers. Your potential customers do not care what you do but care what they obtain from you. Don't get lost giving your clients technical explanations they will not understand, just tell them in plain terms what they will get by doing business with you. For example, our web designer should not rely on technical explanations, but on visual examples of his previous designs. If you learn to identify problems and offer solutions, you've unearthed a diamond mine.

Stumbling block # 5: Neglecting the commercial action. The secret to sales is continuing commercial activity. You gain visibility in your market when your potential client has been exposed to your offer half a dozen times. And your name must come up automatically when clients need your product or service. If they hear your name only one or two times, they'll forget it. Use all the marketing techniques to gain added visibility. In our example, when a company needs web design services, they'll hire the one that they're familiar with because the web designer made sure his name and phone number were visible. They have to feel that they need him.

Stumbling block # 6: Giving up prematurely. Persistence is the key to success in all fields. Set a goal, draw a plan, and then do something every day that will take you there. It works day in and day out. Entrepreneurship is a marathon, not a sprint - it's the kind of sport that favours the athlete who puts in the most effort. Starting a personal business requires the most discipline in the world.

I firmly believe that discipline is the highest form of self-esteem. If you love yourself, you'll take action. Your reward comes when your business starts to work on its own after you've financially secured it and systematised it. In just a few seconds you'll know what it means to systematise.

The list could go on, but what I've mentioned so far should be sufficient for you to start.

38

System, System, System!

EVERY MORNING you get up and go to your business, to your own money-making machine. You turn on the ignition and it starts. In the evening, you go to it again and turn it off until the next day. Are you interested in this kind of arrangement? I am sure the answer is yes, so I will address what's on your mind. You're wondering, *how can this be*? My answer: by creating a perfect system.

Definition # 1: *It's a set of interrelated processes that contribute to an orderly outcome.*

What an idea! Yes, a system is a process that is replicated over and over to create the same result. A fully operational system is an asset (and an asset puts money in your pocket). Systematising a business makes it less and less dependent on the owner. A system does not depend ultimately on people, but on those procedures put in place by whoever controls them.

Definition # 2: *It's talent that's transformed into a service that becomes a source of unlimited income.*

A perfect system is a perfect business. The "perfect business" is a "system" that produces results even without the entrepreneur. The ultimate goal of a good deal or system is to free its owner and finance the lifestyle he wants.

A system is governable. When it no longer is governable, some choose to reduce the size of the business so it becomes governable again. Example: some personal businesses grow chaotically to the point that it drives the owner "mad". He finally decides to take the initial stage of simplifying it - just him. He completed a round trip that was wasted. It's a shame.

I like the word "system" because it is free from the prejudices related to the word "business". At first you work for the system; later, it works for you.

Be smart. Create a system and go to sleep. Better yet, create another system. Collect them like people collect plates or key rings or champagne corks.

The first stage is to systematise, the second stage is to grow it, and the third stage is to replicate it. System - growth - replication. That's it!

An example of systematisation is taken from Michael Dell, founder of Dell Computers. He devised a new way to sell computers - via the Internet (e-commerce), via telephone, or upon the request of clients. This system eliminates the need for intermediaries. It saves the cost of having stores, distributors, and stocks. As a result of this system, his business is one of the leading manufacturers of PCs today, he's one of the wealthiest business owners these days.

A perfect system does not need the owner to be present at all times, since the system is supposed to work on its own. If a person's presence is imperative in a business, it means that it is an imperfect system. If that person ceases to be essential, the business is a perfect business. It is one thing to own a business and another to work in the business.

Consider this basic idea: a perfect system is synonymous with financial freedom. In economic terms, it is a money-making machine; in terms of freedom, it is independence. Your perfect business should not depend on any specific person, much less you.

Entrepreneurs who have not perfected their system need to work hard as managers, not realising that they actually are self-employed under the appearance or illusion of being a business owner.

The key is to work in the system to improve the product or service. The heart of the system should be the process, not the owner. This is the paradigm of financial freedom: to create and own a system that works for its owner and not the reverse.

Companies are flourishing worldwide where they can have administrative tasks performed by a virtual assistant (VA). This virtual assistant, as the name suggests, works remotely from another country for a very interesting price per hour - about $10 / hour. Some virtual assistants charge more, some less.

What administrative tasks are we talking about? Translations, accounting, tax preparation, multimedia presentations, Internet commerce, call centre, marketing and advertising, documentation, web management, database management... It's great to get up in the morning and find an e-mail from your virtual assistant saying all the tasks were completed (while you were sleeping).

If you're interested, you can find a virtual assistant in *International Virtual Association Assistants* (www.ivaa.org). They provide back office services (before and after the sale of products). In adition I hire talent on www.elance.com

The formula for creating a system is to "keep it simple". The simpler the better. So simple that it doesn't need you. Okay, I know from experience that doing this is difficult, but it is entirely possible. To achieve this we need to work **on** the business and not **in** the business. I'll tell you why - there's a huge difference:

Working in the business is being self employed and being part of the system. Hence, you have no freedom. All you have is just work and more work. On the other hand, working on the business is refining the system so that the owner is not needed to continuously operate it. That equates to freedom.

To create a perfect system, work on your business with the ultimate goal of selling it. You heard right. What will happen eventually is that the system will work for you and not the other way around. Your goal is to be dispensable in your personal business.

Having a business is not the same as having a business-employment. For example, being the manager of a restaurant is not the same as being the head chef, waiter, and dishwasher at the same time. If you had to choose between them, what role would you rather play? Take the example of **IBM**. When they started, they spent more time developing the business than doing actual business. They not only engaged in business, they actually built a great business (more than 100 years making bussiness).

This brings me now to franchising. What is the advantage of franchising? Franchises are highly systematised: they know exactly what to do and how to do it - at all times and in all phases of the business. It is also a procurement system that allows economies of scale (which are out of reach of small businesses). Therefore, 75% to 90% of franchises are profitable. The same can't be said for non-franchised businesses, 80% of which close after the first five years. The reason they close is - you guessed it - the lack of a system.

Any personal business, is likely to be systematised (including yours, yes yours). An employee may systematise his or her work, a professional may systematise his or her profession, and an entrepreneur, his business.

But the ego plays tricks, especially on owners who want to feel they're indispensable and then get caught in their own trap. It's like falling on the hole you just dug. Unfortunately, many self-employed entrepreneurs work hard endlessly until they reach the point of exhaustion. Over time, some give up out of sheer exhaustion. Perhaps it wasn't a bad deal; it was just a bad system. When working on your business, ensure that it doesn't rob you of your life.

Remember this keyword: systematise. Once you've absorbed this concept, you can start thinking at the same level as successful people.

39

Profitable Management of Your Time

PEOPLE ACTUALLY COMPLAIN MORE about lack of time than lack of money. The truth is that time is more precious due to its scarcity. If you lose money it can be recovered, but time spent never comes back. And hence it's valuable.

An entrepreneur can use time in the past, present or future. Engaging in the past is to work in accounting, for instance. Dealing with the present is to manage the day to day. Engaging in the future is to design strategies and new revenue streams.

For an entrepreneur, what is more important? Using time for the future is the most important because the first two can be delegated to others. Which of the three occupations use up more time? Depending on your answer, your business is either going backwards, is stagnant, or moving forward.

I've said that it becomes very suspicious when all work schedules require 8 hours a day. Isn't that a weird coincidence? Does all of the world's work require the same number of hours? I don't think so.

I have an argument supporting the arbitrariness of such a schedule. Pareto's law states, "20% of your time creates 80% of your results."

In other words, for a compliance level of 80%, only 20% of the day is sufficient. The rest goes into details. There are 100 minutes a day, that's enough, but it has to be one hundred intense minutes which entail doing only what really counts. And what about the rest of the day? The minutes are spent paper-pushing, answering e-mails, meeting, talking and talking...

I'll ask you: How do you eat a dinosaur? Answer: by making small bites.

Secret #1: Break down a major project into small tasks and you will finish it.

Secret #2: Delegate the small tasks of the major project and you will finish it.

May the dinosaur rest in peace.

In my case, I had to learn to manage my schedule because it was getting complicated. As it was easy to anticipate and think what to do the next week, I learned to focus on the here and now. *"One day every day, one thing at a time."* That's my mantra. It sounds very Zen - and it is. It has saved me from going mad. I recommend it. The job gets easier when you take it in small sips. One step at a time.

Delegate when you can. An excess number of tasks is better than having a lack of tasks. Yes, I know. Nobody does it better than you, but what bags the Oscar is not perfection, it's what you pursue - your freedom. You can delegate the 80% of tasks that make the 20% of your results. Those are your underperforming tasks. You're leaving the 20% to your partners, while you earn 80% of your time!

"It is not enough to be busy... the question is: what are we busy on?" (Henry David Thoreau). It is not doing more, but doing what counts.

The manuals and courses that are designed to do more in less time are a failure. Some always seek them hoping to discover a secret to getting more hours than they have. Impossible. Even if it were possible, it would ultimately fall short. Being busy does not mean anything if your time is taken up by things that aren't right. Many people do unnecessary tasks. How do I know that? Because they do not lead anywhere. It's like running on a treadmill that does not lead anywhere except towards exhaustion. In the end, everything relies on using available time to do the important tasks.

Divide the day into compartments of tasks. In the morning do one thing, and in the afternoon another. I dedicate all my mornings to those issues that would make a difference in my profession: planning, writing books, learning, promoting myself. In the evening, I take to the podium: giving courses, conducting coaching sessions, doing lectures, and granting media interviews. Half of my day is spent developing my model, the second half is spent working on it: organising & planning.

Results of one survey revealed that 72% said they did not plan their time because they just didn't "have time." Can you believe it?

Ask this question and write the answer: How do I best use my next hour? Your journey should not consist of more than two priorities - two major issues per day.

Results or tasks? To me it's clear. What about you? Is it clear to you? The entrepreneur is not seeking to be busy, he's seeking results. R-e-s-u-l-t-s.

For example, I didn't write a book (considered a task), I built and developed a best seller (considered the outcome). Do you see the difference between tasks and results?

Replace your tasks with results and then see how it makes you more efficient... Results are important. Tasks are usually urgent but not necessarily important. For example, a ringing telephone is urgent because it has to be answered, but it isn't significant (it could be a wrong number or a routine call). The moral lesson here is: the noise and toning it down are urgent tasks, but silence is important.

Ask yourself: *Am I putting the important tasks ahead of the urgent ones?*

Use your agenda and distribute your projects over some months. If you take the whole year and write down - every month - milestones you intend to accomplish, you will have an overview of what to expect in any given year.

Assigning dates is important. *"A goal without a plan is just a wish"* Antoine de Saint-Exupéry said. And allow me to add this: *"A goal without a date is just an idea."*

Protect your time. Learning to say "no" is the pinnacle of self-esteem. When you say "yes" but actually mean "no", you are actually saying "no" to yourself. How long can you sustain this? Not too long. I saw tears and heartaches over this issue. Love yourself more. Learn to say "no" when you mean "no".

Some time wasters: e-mails without rhyme or reason, messages with power points and music, unnecessary meetings, unjustified travel, walk-ins, paperwork, absurd, endless phone calls, conversations in the hallway with people who do not know what to do, intolerable interruptions...

You don't want these time wasters, do you? Your time is too valuable. If you don't believe me, ask your family who barely sees you.

Make a list of things to avoid. And then put a title to your list: "My policy." If you tell someone you cannot do what they're asking because it goes against "your professional policy" they will respect it without discussions. No one discusses or questions the "house policy." Nothing personal, it's a standard that works - all the time.

Focus on what's important. Be relentless about this. What is the most important thing you could do to achieve the greatest impact on your purpose? If a task does not take you a little closer to your goal, it is not worth it. Discard it.

Apply the problem-solving technique: "Touch Paper Once": when a paper lands on your desk you have three options: solve it, delegate it to someone, or recycle it in the trash. In case of doubt, the third option is the right one.

Charge by project, not by hour. Whenever possible, the better method is to charge a fixed fee for the project rather than counting the hours and multiplying them by a price per hour. Your customers want to buy results or solutions to their problems, not your time. Your service is your talent, and it should not be counted in terms of hours. A conductor charges by the hour? That means he's not charging for his performance. Does Tom Hanks charge by the hour? Of course not, he charges per film.

How about you? Do you charge by the hour or by the project?

Good management of time does not focus in doing more in less time, but in doing what matters with more talent. Performance is measured in talent applied, not time spent. Throw your watch away.

I wrote this section to save and safeguard your time because it is your greatest wealth. Michael Landon, star of the television series "Little House on the Prairie", once said: *"Somebody should tell us, right at the beginning of our lives, that we are dying. Then we could live every second of every day."* That's something to think about. Here's another favourite quote: *"Time is more valuable than money. You can get more money, but you cannot get more time."* (Jim Rohn, motivational speaker)

40

Common "Shipwrecks"

THERE ARE ERRORS IN MANUALS, textbooks, even in songs...they are predictable and can be avoided from the beginning.

Pay attention to the following list of common mistakes and you avoid 90% of the causes of "shipwrecks". Avoid these icebergs if you don't want to convert your personal business into a sinking Titanic on her maiden voyage. Many projects and initiatives do not survive their first year. I do not want this to happen to you. By the time you finish reading this section, you will have learned to overcome the obstacles experienced by the majority.

Iceberg # 1. Neglecting your financial education. It is impossible to be in business without knowing basic financial concepts. Read the economic and business sections of your paper, read magazines published for entrepreneurs, businesses and franchises, take a course on investing and management, follow business gurus, read biographies of successful entrepreneurs.

You wouldn't haggle with your doctor on what he prescribes for you, would you? Train yourself by listening to lectures on finance. No one has to ask you if you like it or not, it's a must! Imagine that you have a queue waiting their turn, but I suggest that you add some of the above to your list of suggestions pending. Your economy will thank you!

Iceberg # 2. Buying without evaluating the alternatives. You earn money by buying well, not selling well. I think it's so important to spend time to evaluate the purchase of assets, products or services just as it is important in selling them. Convert each purchase into an act of financial intelligence. Ask yourself: "Who - or what -will pay for this purchase?" If you're paying, forget it, it's an expense. If your business or your customers are paying, go ahead, it's an investment.

Iceberg # 3. Not having an emergency fund or a "financial air-bag." Build a reserve fund for your financial freedom", a financial cushion that will cover a year of your current expenses in case you lose your main source of income. Comfortable with the thought of having "batteries" for the next 12 months gives you a sense of serenity (this applies to both employees and entrepreneurs).

The emergency fund should cover between 3 and 12 months, depending on what it costs to replace your income. Having a reserve for 24 months would be great. If you have a good backup, you will go to work much more relaxed and with less pressure; if things go bad, you have a whole year of resources you can count on.

Iceberg # 4. Not having cash. I learned in banking that good companies work with their own money, i.e. funds that the company generates. Your cash flow should be positive, and must generate the necessary funds to meet payments, is a matter of square box with the calendar. Economies that do not add liquidity to the payment dates, suspend payments.

Iceberg # 5. Thinking and acting like a self-employed person rather than as an entrepreneur. Prosperity is not money but a way of thinking. Each role (employee, self-employed, entrepreneur) presupposes a different way of thinking and acting. If a person changes his role without changing his mindset, problems are bound to occur. The disparity between what it is and what it is doing is a cause of many shipwrecks.

Iceberg # 6. Reaching the point of exhaustion. Working more hours than necessary and doing non-essential tasks are a perfect recipe for personal and financial disaster. In Japan, they already have a name for the overworking disease - *karoshi*. Many self-employed persons are so busy working that they have little or no time to manage their business. The entrepreneur's role is to design a perfect business system that will free him more and more.

Iceberg # 7. Not having a good accounting system. Having the information at the right time is everything. I've met people who do not know, or can't even approximate how much they earn (or lose). They are far from controlling their personal business. Subcontract your accounting tasks it to an accountant you trust. Try to devote a little time each week to analysing your income and expenses using a spreadsheet.

Iceberg # 8. Spending because there is excess cash. Cash surpluses are not to be spent or distributed. It is one thing to spend and another thing to have to spend. Since every Euro of profit you earned required work and time, find a place where you can put every Euro earned. Put it to work for you. Declare every dollar your "Employee of the Month". And don't let go of the money so easily, your job is to give the best possible job to your money, you are his "employer", make it work for you.

Iceberg # 9. Diverting money from your business to your personal life. Some people confuse their personal finances with their businesses. They are not the same. As a result of this confusion, expenditures often deviate from one financial situation to another which leads to a distorted reality. Sometimes, the first income from a business goes to financing personal expenses when they should be reinvested in the business. Let me help you with this. The first thing you should do is to set up different bank accounts.

Iceberg # 10. Not reinvesting the profits of your business. A business grows with the business' cash flow. Self-financing should be a priority. Simply put, a business must pay for itself and then provide a surplus for the owner. If the funds generated by the business leave the company, you will soon need external financing via loans, increasing your interest expense. This puts the business in a vulnerable and precarious situation.

Iceberg # 11. Needing the first year's revenue. If an entrepreneur wants a salary, he's better off finding a job. The entrepreneur does not live on a salary but on benefits. He is not interested in a fixed salary, but in creating assets that will earn much more than a pay check.

For example, Bill Gates is not the highest paid man in the world and that is why he is the world's richest man. Steve Jobs of Apple set an annual salary of one dollar for himself. Yes, one sad dollar covered his pay for 12 months. Because I love the variables, that's hundreds of millions of dollars annually on results. Make no mistake; you have to earn them...

Iceberg # 12. Not having competent consultants for accounting, legal issues, IT matters, and tax specialists. Your personal business will be excellent if the employees are too. A business is a reflection of its owner, its customers, suppliers, and partners. There is nothing more dangerous than believing that you are well advised when in fact you're not. Another common mistake in particular is to hire a consultant and not pay attention to his or her recommendations.

Iceberg # 13. Having an excess of success. The lack of success kills a business and the opposite is also true. Too much success can kill a business. To not re-invent yourself when everything is going well is dangerous because unlimited success is a fantasy. If your current personal business is a success, it just means it's time to improve it further or start another.

Reinvent your business every 24 or 36 months. Do not delay or it could smell musty. We all need to go down and go up in the process of construction and deconstruction. Examples of re-inventing could include rewriting your mission, changing your business card, questioning your slogan, improving your marketing, changing all your presentations and your brochures, introducing a new product or service and stripping away some (but still give you money) .

Yes, you read correctly. You better throw it away before you find it in the trash one day. Ohhh! Recycle it. the biggest players do it and they do very well. Picasso: "No construction without destruction."Hallelujah, someone has understood. It's like changing to stay. As Giorgio Armani once said, *"I am convinced that I have reached a point where I start all over from scratch. I have to question myself and rightly so. Starting over is always positive. There's more to come."*

Coco Chanel was also great when she said that to be irreplaceable, one must always be different. Meaning: if you yourself "destroy" your business, you can build one on its ashes, but if the market destroys it, eventually it will destroy you too.

Madonna is an artist of great influence; her virtue is that she reinvents herself frequently. Her image transformations undergo a revolution ahead of the trend and she keeps current through the decades. We know her in different "versions": as an actress, singer, writer, and as a person who is innocent, sassy, punk, profane, sophisticated, blasphemous, maternal, spiritual... Madonna is everything. In a recent "version", she adopted eastern philosophies and the Kabbalah, spending 5 million dollars to create a Kabbalah base in London. Her secret: she reinvents herself constantly to remain in the radar.

41

Learn to Sell (if you're going to be in business)

THIS SECTION CONTAINS proven strategies for promoting yourself as an entrepreneur. None of them costs money and that's something you can appreciate when you're starting out. However, these strategies don't mean that they're free. I will share them with you in a moment.

Rich people focus on selling more, the rest work harder.

Before anything, let me tell you that the problem of a "business" is that it does not do enough of selling. The words "business" and "sale" go hand in hand. They are inseparable. It would be strange if a business thrives without promotion, marketing and sales. There are rare exceptions.

If you want to thrive in your personal business, you must learn to promote it (or hire someone to do it for you if you can afford it).

The first thing to learn about selling is to accept the rejection. The more you reject the rejection, the closer you get to the sale.

I have met excellent professionals - architects, musicians, counsellors, therapists, designers, computer engineers. They excelled in their respective fields, but they were a disaster at promoting themselves. Let's face it, being an "anonymous genius" actually accomplishes little. It's better to identify the genius and share it with the world.

I remember a client who was an extraordinary saxophonist. He spent many hours improving his skill but did nothing to make himself known. Consequently, he couldn't land a job and survived by teaching. During my first coaching session with him, I told him what was happening in his life and he understood. From that time on, he began to advertise more and rehearse less.

Conclusion: he is no longer "the best unknown saxophone player in the country" but he now enjoys the luxury of playing in concerts. He feels recognised and at the same time, his audience enjoys his talent. Everyone is happy. Moral lesson: perfection is useless if nobody enjoys it. Stop being an anonymous genius!

Promotion and selling skills lie at the heart of financial success. *"Everyone lives by selling something"* said writer Robert Louis Stevenson. I hope you agree with me that we all sell, we all work in sales, whether as employees or as entrepreneurs.

We do not sell a product or service. What we sell are the benefits of a product or service. We sell solutions to problems.

What problems do you solve? In the next few minutes, you will discover that the larger the problems you solve, the more money will come to you. This is why I say that a big problem is a great opportunity for anyone. The expert problem solvers have people at the door with money in hand, willing to pay someone to help solve their problems.

Key: look for big problems, roll up your sleeves, and solve them.

Instead of promoting what you do, focus instead on the solutions you provide. Your customers want to hear about benefits and results. Do you see the difference? Sales are lost because the proper arguments were not expressed at the time of selling. Sellers focus on their own reasons for wanting to sell, not on the reasons why a customer needs to buy.

Although I use the words "product" and "service" throughout this book, I think they are obsolete terms (in Spanish we say *"passado el arroz"* which means, they have been cooking too long). The more precise terms would be "benefit" and "solution" respectively.

Stop reading and think. Your customers want you to help them make a profit and /or solve their problems. The rest is banal chatter and they don't care.

~~Product~~ = Benefit
~~Service~~ = Solution

Your clients don't want you to sell to them, they want to buy. Respect their will and facilitate the sale without forcing it. The higher mental state of a seller is mental wealth, from where he does not "need" to make the sale, but prefers making it to not making it.

If you do not need to make the sale, the potential client does not detect your desperation to sell (the poisonous element). Would you buy what the seller is desperate to get rid? Of course not, no one wants what the other "does not want himself."

People do not like us to sell to them. So instead of creating a selling atmosphere, why not create a "purchasing atmosphere"? If your potential customer senses that you want to sell, he will get defensive even if they still need what you're offering. But if you invite them to buy, leaving space for them to make the decision, they will do business with you.

Relax, put aside the need to sell, and everything will flow naturally. Selling is not pushing, persuading or manipulating people to buy from you. Selling is about listening to people and connecting with their needs. The good sale focuses on listening, on asking, on the client's needs. Poor sales focus on speaking, giving advice, and the needs of the seller.

Be smart and promote yourself. How? With the "Entrepreneur Promotion Kit":

✓ Define your "motto". Write a sentence of no more than ten words - one that's easy to remember and creates impact. You can even have several slogans for your services or products. I will give some examples later.

✓ Increase your visibility: do this through blogs, media, talks, articles. If you are "invisible" no one will see you, even if you're very good in your field. For example, having the best website in the world is of little use if you do not generate traffic and visitors, and then compelling them to take action.

✓ Talk to everyone you know about what you do. Include those you don't know. Talk, talk, talk ... It will help you be more outgoing and enable you to make your offer without complications. Sales are a matter of numbers: the more you explain your "business history", the more people will buy. In fact, if you're so proud of your personal business (as you are of your children, showing their photos around often) you might as well discuss your personal business with every living creature that crosses your path!

✓ Formulate your "elevator speech" or your 20-second promotional gig. Write the script of your ad as if you were going to advertise it on TV. Because you only have 20 seconds to do it, you must be very specific and precise in your message. This will help you summarise what your business is so people have a better understanding of what you do. I will give some examples later.

✓ Ask your clients to refer their acquaintances to you. Word-of-mouth is the most effective sales machine in history. Turn them into "evangelists" for your project. Build a social network of people who speak highly of what you do and who recommend you wholeheartedly. This has a cascading effect.

✓ Project an expert image in your field. The best way to do this is to write one or several books. It is not hard to write. How complicated is it to sell to a publisher and especially to the market? Luckily you can now self-publish for a small fee; when you have sold enough copies, publishers will be interested in you. If you want to start with opinion articles, go ahead, it is faster and easier to write them.

THE MONEY CODE

✓ Write catchy ads. Do a search on Joe Vitale on the Internet and get his work "*Hypnotic Writing.*" Watch him work his magic with online marketing. They call him the "Buddha of the Internet." He is also the author of "Spiritual Marketing". He applies hypnosis to commercial messages and the businesses that consult with him succeed.

If you'll notice I did not mention advertising. The costs of advertising are not justified, except in very specific areas. My opinion is that marketing is more powerful than advertising, and in most cases there is no significant cost.

As I promised, let's talk about your "motto". I think it deserves a good discussion. Let's get down to business: A business needs a slogan or motto that defines what it offers and how it can greatly benefit the customer.

Imagine that you're participating in my seminar "*From employee to entrepreneur.*" In this environment of mutual encouragement, I ask you to write your slogan on the back of your professional card. You haven't got much space so be brief. On one side of your card your name appears, and on the other, your slogan. Great. How about sharing it with the other attendees?

My slogan is: "*Coaching to think big*" and "*We play a bigger game.*"

Now let's look at some of the slogans by famous companies:

- The Apple iPod: "1000 songs in your pocket."
- Domino's Pizza: "Hot pizza delivered to your home in 30 minutes."
- Eckhart Tolle: "The world can change only from within."
- Coca-Cola: "The spice of life."
- MRW: "Building trust."
- Starbucks: "A reward for every moment of the day."
- Hay House (Louise Hay): "Look inside."
- Volvo: "Safety first."
- L'Oreal: "Because you're worth it."

See how snappy these slogans are. They're short but brilliant. They appeal to the right brain (the part of the brain that caters to the emotions). Because I'm a writer, I love words and phrases that are short and decisive. They summarise a powerful idea.

Once you've got your slogan or business message clear, it should appear in all of your communications. It's your ice-breaker when selling - your mark of identity in the market. Will it cost anything to write it?

Note: If you can't describe what makes you different and excellent in 25 words or less, don't write it. Take care of your company", said Harry Beckwith in his book "Delight your Clients." You've already heard it.

The other point that we have yet to clarify is, what is meant by "elevator speech"?

Answer: Let's say you're in the elevator and you need to introduce yourself to a person and that you only have a few seconds to do it, while the elevator goes up or down a few floors ... you need to summarise and finalise your introduction about "who you are, what you do, and how you can serve him." It's a way of speaking because, in reality, your "elevator speech" is your professional presentation, a social act...

Here is my example of an "elevator speech" (you were expecting it, right?)

"Do you know how a person feels if he has not achieved the biggest dream of his life? I think you do. During my courses, I dedicate my efforts to supporting the dreams of people who want to give meaning to their lives."

In my seminar, *"The money code"*, each participant develops his "elevator speech". They share ideas in a group, and inspire one another. You can instantly feel the enthusiasm and energy in the room.

42

Catchy Ads that Sell

IF YOU'RE GOING to put an ad, the following can help you do it effectively. I've been wasting a lot of money on ads, because they have a bad approach. Or they don't always work, or aren't useful for all types of activities. I have some guidelines to offer you. Fasten your safety belt, we're about to take off and learn how you can influence your market.

You decide that you want to advertise. Your ideal ad requires a title and subtitle, both of which reflect the best advantages of your offer. The body of your message must mention the other benefits of that can be derived from your offer. Be specific and brief. Do not explain what you do or how you do it in any part of your ad or anywhere else because these are features of your product or service; your potential clients are only interested in the advantages or benefits of your offer.

Remember that the characteristics or features of a product or service go directly to the mind of a consumer, whereas the benefits appeal to the heart or emotion. One goes the logical route (the brain) and the other to the emotional route. What do you think would sell more?

For example, if you're going to the bank, which of these two messages would interest you more?

1. *You will make an annual guaranteed rate of 7% - 70 Euros for every thousand.*
2. *You will invest into a structured deposit - for a fixed and variable term indexed to the evolving weighted average for 3 years of three Nasdaq-indexed technology securities, enjoying annual yields of return.*

In reading these, even I am still trying to understand the second one, so I'll go with the first. It appeals directly to my portfolio.

Let's go to the bottom of the ad is the ideal section for a call to action: sign up, call, buy, make a reservation, ask for an interview, request additional information, go to a meeting ... The ad must always generate an action and indicate to the reader how to proceed.

If you want to arouse the interest of your potential customer:

- Tell people that you have the answers to their questions and the solution to their problem. Be sincere when you say this.
- Tell them to take concrete action. Don't limit yourself to just informing them, but also motivate them to take decisions and act. Indicate what the next step is.
- Show the benefits and advantages of your offer in the form of a list.
- Lead them to their right brain: that part of the brain that is emotional, intuitive, and sensitive. Actions are taken based on emotion, not on logical reason.
- Use metaphors to explain something in terms of another thing so that they understand; use similes to compare two ideas so they illustrate your message better; use testimonials (from well-known people) to reinforce your message. Metaphors, similes, testimonials.
- Stress the usefulness and simplicity of your offer. Simplify the lives of others.

- Write your messages in colloquial language, as though you're writing a letter to another person.
- Let your passion and conviction shine in what you're doing. Nothing convinces others more than enthusiasm.
- Convey a tone of authority - like you're an expert in your field based on your own experience. Your testimonials received from others will communicate much more than what you can say.

Your perfect ad will reach the ideal client, capture his attention and interest, provide value, establish credibility; it describes how you stand out from your competition, focuses on the benefits to your client, and ends with a call to action.

43

Multi-level Marketing Option

MULTI-LEVEL MARKETING (MLM) companies represent an opportunity to start your own business. You work within a network and you receive the support and training that are more important. This option eliminates a lot of the steps in the process of creating a business because there is nothing more you need when you start distributing (the product or service). It's one of the business models that has grown rapidly - more than others. It's as revolutionary as the franchise model which today is used all over the world.

What products or services can you sell? Numerous! Cosmetics, communications, games, clothes, food supplements, financial services, software... -300 companies- some better, some worst, like in everything. It is estimated that in the United States alone, some 15 million people receive income from multi-level marketing, and about 60 million in the rest of the world. Many baby boomers, who will be retiring in the next few years, go into multi-level marketing to supplement their retirement incomes.

There's an infinite number of products that are being distributed through multi-level marketing, although I perceive that there are advantages to selling nutritional supplements in particular because:

(a) almost everyone is interested in them, (b) they are consumed daily, (c) they are priced such that they cater to all budgets, and (d) clients can prove the benefits first hand.

The work consists of speaking (and partly recommending) about a product in which you believe in blindly because it's been tried and tested before and more importantly, it works for you. You like it so much that you cannot stop talking about its advantages with everyone. We know that a client's enthusiasm conveys more than any ad published by a company. It is sufficient to say that you know how this product changed your life in some way. If the person who receives the comment decides to test it himself, he only has to place his order by phone, and the company will send the product (and the commission to the person who recommended it). There's no paper work, no stock, no product handling, no money involved. The next step is to create a network of sub-distributors who make their own sales. The distributor who sponsors them also receives a commission from the company.

Given that are many MLM options, consider these factors before you decide which one you'd try:

1. The quality of the product
2. The company's reputation
3. The frequency of use of the product
4. The compensation plan

Multi-level marketing is a way of doing business that is not so well-known because it is not visible: there are no specific locations, no advertising, no stores, no financing, and no employees. But the most important thing about it is that it generates passive income. You already know that passive income is that which will repeat itself tomorrow, and day after day, for something that you did yesterday.

Let me say it one more time: passive or residual income will make you free. It's the income of the rich.

Despite these advantages, very few see the opportunity because they only see what they are prepared to see. Prejudices exist about multi-level marketing, and because of lack of knowledge, it is identified with pyramid schemes. It's an absurd fear that stems from ignorance.

A network is much more powerful than an individual working solo. Multilevel marketing provides leverage, thanks to a network of contacts.

The more participants there are in a network, the better its value. Metcalf's Law sums it up: "The economic value of a network grows exponentially, not arithmetically. The power of the network is based on "viral marketing": recommend a product to a person, who in turn makes it known to someone else, and in turn that someone else refers it yet to a third person ...

As an example, social networks like Facebook increase their usefulness and value when it has more participants. Another example: a franchise increases its power as the number of franchisees grows in the market.

You already know that word-of-mouth is the best marketing technique. Maybe one day there will be a better way to market, but it still has not been invented. MLM uses this huge leverage as a distribution strategy. And the best way to increase the number of recommendations that a company receives is very simple: ask for them. Don't wait for it, don't pray that they come. Instead ask for it specifically: "*Would you be willing to recommend me to people you know?*" And asking this is so quick; it's not difficult, right? If you don't ask for it, how will they know that you want them to recommend you? They can't read your mind, they're not fortune tellers, help them to help you.

Say it clearly: *I want to serve more clients the way I served you.* This habit duplicates your rate of recommendations, allowing you to double your income. The Biblical saying "Ask and it shall be given to you" should be the first chapter of any sales manual.

To illustrate the power of a recommendation: TV personality Oprah Winfrey started a programme - The Oprah Book Club. She selects a book, reads it, is impressed by it, and then comments on it and recommends it on the air. Well, of the 46 books she presented in her programme's first season - all - yes all - became a best seller! Such is the power of recommendation.

Multi-level marketing has numerous advantages: it requires minimal or no investment. There are no debts, no facilities or inventories, no employees, no product handling, no unpaid goods; the hours are flexible and it provides passive income streams indefinitely. It is also a great business school. It teaches you to promote, sell, communicate, work in teams, think like a business owner and collaborate in a competitive atmosphere. Without risking your money, it offers you the possibility of creating your own distribution network. It can always be the start of other businesses.

The only drawback I have experienced is that neither the product nor the company belongs to you. Statistics reveal that 90% of the people starting an MLM business give it up eventually because of their lack of involvement, persistence, and discipline. Since it does not cost you anything to get in, getting out is also easy. Easy come, easy go. At the slightest difficulty, you give up.

Multilevel marketing is a way of working smarter rather than working harder, for a simple reason: the power of leveraging is the sum of the efforts of a network wherein everyone wins.

44

"I", registered trademark

LET me remind you that your personal business requires its own identity to survive in your market. It is known as "positioning yourself." If you're not sure what your market position is, then no one else will. So, roll up your sleeves, and go re-invent your personal brand. You need to re-invent yourself each time, you're like a work in progress because you're always "building" your talents.

Your personal brand is more than your name, more than your legal status; it is, in fact, the DNA of your project. All of your decisions must contribute towards building it and making your market remember it. If you don't have it, no one will see you!

Whatever your talent is, transform it into a brilliant offer. I'm talking about being great - brilliant - in what you do. Remember these five words:

> Be great in what's yours.

Your personal brand differentiates you; it is the summary of your talents. Obama has it, Madonna has it, Judge Garzón has it, and Rafa Nadal has it. It therefore does not matter that you have a company or you are an independent professional, civil servant, self-employed worker, politician, athlete, artist or a creative worker - your personal brand is one of your most important assets.

When you do a presentation or give a sales meeting, you are actually "selling" to yourself. Only when you have achieved credibility can you close the sale of the product or service you're offering. Some bad sellers skip this step and immediately close the sale and botch it up. No one will buy from you unless they trust you and consider you as the appropriate person to do business with. For this reason, your first sale is "selling" yourself as a professional.

But:

Can you become brilliant in something that does not excite you?

Do you get medals for doing something half-heartedly?

Do you know of a millionaire who hates what he does?

Answers: no, no, and definitely no. The first condition for success is to be excited and passionate in what you do, and then and only then, will people become excited as you. The money follows. Always in that order. I'm not the one who's saying this, but multi-millionaire Malcolm Forbes said it to his son: *"don't go to work for just one day, do something that you really like to do, and then you'll be the richest of men."* That is a financial education, and it is clear that it counts as an advantage. Echo is a wonderful metaphor that teaches us that "what goes around comes around." With passion it's the same - we can't wait for it without first offering it.

Passion is the wind that powers the sails of any good business.

"Do it with all your heart, and prosper" (from the Bible, Chronicles II)

Your heart will tell you what your ideal occupation is. It's your compass, follow it. Write your "declaration of love" in your notebook. Be sincere with it, don't lie or try to be proper or to please anyone, it is your life and you alone choose what to do with it, it will be 100% for you.

Too many people have "resigned themselves internally"; that is, engaging too long in occupations that have ceased to be interesting. Yet they continue in these occupations to keep their income. They limit themselves to doing the minimum expected of them so they don't get fired, and since it pays enough they hold on to it.

Apathy is a step back for all humans. These attitudes ruin their financial situation, and constitute moral ruin for everyone. No society has ever progressed or advanced with indifference and lack of interest. Unwillingness is a waste of work, and the contribution that can be made is lost. A company evolves towards success or failure by the collective thinking of all its members. When their thinking is negative, they cheat themselves of happiness, satisfaction, passion, and finally they lose their jobs because suddenly there is someone else who wishes to perform the job with genuine commitment.

The above is not a theory, it happened to me, and is happening now in many parts of the world.

45

Promote Yourself

QUESTION: What do you do? The wrong response is to mention a generic profession: lawyer, businessman, self-employed worker, speech therapist, transporter, professor, dentist, consultant... It makes me dizzy thinking of it. Even worse is to respond mentioning one's degree: licensed biologist, optical studies graduate, first mechanic, Master's in Business Administration...

As far as I know, no one is a profession, nor an academic title! We are people, professionals with training, and engaged in a profession, I agree, but we're neither of these.

So how do we present or introduce ourselves? It's better to mention the problems that you solve. You will create a greater impact on your speaker if you follow this recommendation before giving him petty answers that bore him to death.

In marketing, it is a mortal sin not to differentiate your offer. What's different about being an engineer? A musician? Nothing at all, if you keep it clear in your mind that you are unique. Generic answers definitely don't sell. It brings about a laconic "Ahh", from the other person and he moves on. I'll bet a Euro that the person you just met will think: "oh, another one of those." He'll forget you - forever. What horror.

Can you afford to lose an opportunity to promote yourself? I don't think so. Jack Trout, a management expert, said, *"If you're not different, it's better to charge a very low price."* Some entrepreneurs believe that their service or product cannot be differentiated, and this is not true. Even if it is identical to what others are offering, the packaging context can change radically. For example, you wouldn't know the difference between the tea that is served in the airport cafeteria and the one in an exclusive lounge with a Zen atmosphere. It's the same tea - and from the same supplier!

Create an emotional connection with your client. The target goal of the buyer is not the purchase itself, but it is his emotional state at the time of purchase. I'm not sure that Apple sells computers, perhaps it's selling experience. Geez, there are emotions and design issues at play here. Have you not yet realised their competence? They are determined to make PCs look mediocre (like ugly dark boxes)?

In 1960, Rosser Reeves, an advertising man, coined the concept: "unique selling proposition" (the acronym: U.S.P.) and it consists of a brief but powerful promotional message that includes:

- identifying your market and target client (make a list of the characteristics of your ideal client).
- defining the most important problem that you solve for clients (make a list of the major problems that you solve for clients).
- the principal benefits that you've achieved for your clients (make a list of the main benefits that you offer to your clients).
- the irresistible desire of your potential client to learn more (make a list of questions frequently asked and your answers).

All in one paragraph. Wow! You'll have to sharpen your pencil ... and summarise how your offer is different.

I can give you my example: *"Do you know how a person behaves when he feels limited and blocked? My commitment is to break down their internal resistance - teaching them - like a renowned author in my field - to think big and to help bring out the greatness that resides in them."*

Now, it's your turn. Take paper and pencil and write down your USP (at the back of your card)

Let me help you by providing this diagram:

P
Promise

Include a promise that appeals to the emotions of people.

U
Unique

Explain how you're different from the rest, something that only you can provide.

S
Sales

Add the main benefit that your customer gains by doing business with you.

When your USP is clearly stated, you can always use it in your daily conversations with anyone you meet. Remember to get to know a potential client each day (you never know beforehand who they are). It's like playing "blind man's buff" with those around you - there are persons who can be your clients! But to discover who they are, you have to arouse their interest with a brilliant offer.

It's a game, and it's fun!

Got it? Have you caught the idea? Let's now give the screw another half twist turn.

The USP is good, but the HSP is even better. What is HSP? It means "Holistic Sales Proposal (HSP). It goes far beyond the usefulness of the product or service and enhances the context with which it is presented to the client. Examples include: social commitment, warranty policy, packaging, corporate ethics, stationery, décor, the language used in business.

The game grows and becomes better, and still is fun.

Context is essential; the way a product is packaged and wrapped (also called product envelope) is equally essential.

Two years ago, Joshua Bell, a virtuoso violinist, carried out an experiment in the Washington metro. With his instrument - a valuable 1730 Stradivarius - he played classical tunes for 43 minutes. It must be mentioned that people have to pay at least $100.00 to listen to his performance in a hall.

In that Washington metro experiment, of the 1,070 people who came up to him, only 27 gave money; the majority of them did not stop to listen to him. A total of $32.00 was received during that 43-minute period. Only one person - a lover of rock - stopped and stayed six minutes to listen to him.

Who says now that context doesn't matter? The same musician, the same violin, the same pieces, the same talent ... these would cost much more in the Boston Symphony Hall.

The product or service "envelope" is worth just as much as the actual product or service. Sometimes, more.

46

Building a Website that Sells

IN THIS SECTION, you will discover the Code of the e-rich.

Start by telling yourself that to be in business, you need a website that's focused on creating value. After visiting your website, your visitors must feel that they have to do something and you must tell them what it is they should do. I wrote this book to tell you that it is not the complexity of the design, but the effectiveness, that you should think about when you build a website so that it generates earnings.

Today's websites embody pre-historic notions of what lies ahead. These days, websites are silly, flat, one-dimensional, frozen: there is no interaction with the visitor, they ignore his preferences, they don't recognise him, they always offer him the same cover. Moreover, they are not proactive, are not business-like, and they don't close the sale or monitor results... This is about to change, and it will change a lot.

What we can do in the meantime is to test our present website rudiments and attract the search engines in order to have intelligent websites. We will have a virtual persuasive sales person on the web, someone who's unique, the best of the best - for no pay.

Build a website that sells. Your website shouldn't get the award for web design, nor should it be limited to becoming just an online pamphlet about the network. It is not a digital ad, it must be more than that. Provide reasons so that your potential public visits your website (offer information of value, useful resources, interesting links, a gift, various offers...) And once they're there, encourage them to add your site to their list of favourites and to sign up for your newsletters.

What are the three main goals of your website?

1. *Visibility and Accessibility*. Let them see you. Better yet: make them meet you. In the construction trade, the key is location. In online business, the key is visitor traffic. A website without traffic is like an ad in the dark side of the moon. Your job is to provide visitor traffic to your website, and to convert visitors into clients who become fans of your product or service. For all of this to happen, the visitor to your website must feel that he has landed in Shangri-la and that the screen of his computer gives him access to a gold mine.
2. *Credibility and Authority*. Position yourself as a point of reference in your market - an expert. Your market's perception is everything. That said, we have all visited websites that are too diversified in their offers; they lose credibility because "*they're all over the map.*" It is much better to concentrate on your unique selling proposal (USP) in a well-defined area. If you want to offer more or to diversify, create other distinct websites.
3. *Access and Interaction*. Each page of your web site must contain at least one call to action. Myour visitors to do something: call you, write you, sign up for your newsletter, buy online, recommend your site, come to see you, feel a desire to know more ... in short, your visitors must take action.

As kids, we played in stores and found it exciting, didn't we? Today, anyone can have his own store online. Remember when people were at first suspicious of ATMs (automatic teller machines) and preferred to do their banking in person? Today it is ridiculous to not trust ATMs. The same thing happened with online shopping; there was reluctance at first; with time, however, shopping on the Internet will make up the bulk of commercial transactions. For this reason I think that all businesses should have an online store.

PS: I hope you are convinced now that not having a website is a mistake. I hope I have also convinced you that you can transform your website into a passive income machine 24 hours a day, 7 days a week, 365 days a year. It's the same as telling you that you can transform your computer into an automatic cash machine.

47

Your Online Service Providers

ONE OF THE secrets of Internet success is to rely on good online service providers (O.S.P.). These are companies (or individuals) that open doors for you to the global market, allowing you to systematise your business. You can contract out programmes, services, memory space - all that you need at a low monthly fee. Companies that provide domain names and web hosting are one example. A few years ago, registering a domain name cost 50 Euros a year; these days it costs 10 Euros a year and you receive a package of supplementary utilities with this service.

Online service providers are responsible for providing the technologies your project needs. You're an entrepreneur and you don't have to be a computer expert, nor do you have to buy all of the applications you use. Instead of creating or buying this technology, you can rent it for a modest fee. Wouldn't it much better to invest in your business than invest continuously in technology?

OSP companies will facilitate design software for entrepreneurs wishing to run their personal businesses from home, or for micro businesses, or for offices of professionals. You use the same technologies used by large companies. The outsourcing revolution has arrived! It's like sub-contracting the IT department at a low cost.

If you don't want to hand over the responsibility of your website to a professional web master, you can create your own website through an OSP. For a small monthly or annual fee, you can - without any programming knowledge - use their existing templates and have your own space with sufficient memory in their servers for hosting your website. It's an inexpensive and quick option allowing you to test your business online. If at a later time you want a more professional website, you can always hire someone to do it, although it will be at a higher cost.

Axiom: those professionals who are capable of taking advantage of new technologies will have nothing to fear in the new global economy. But first, they have to get accustomed with the rapid pace of technological change.

Hop onto the technology change bandwagon or be crushed by it!

48

Your Irresistible Internet Marketing

ALL OF US have heard the word Marketing - a series of actions you take that attract clients to your business.

I consider marketing a lot more interesting than advertising. The first is active (creativity in action), the second is passive (pay for an ad and wait for results). Furthermore, advertising is expensive and does not always cover the costs. If an entrepreneur believes that marketing is only for large companies and not for a personal business, he'll miss out on viable opportunities.

There are four basic areas in marketing (the four Ps): *product, positioning, price and promotion*. I agree that it sounds trite and maybe even minimalist, but it works. Sit with your team and define each of these areas. Don't neglect any of them; otherwise, your efforts will not generate the desired results.

Your multiple income system must think of the e-money option (online income). For this, it is necessary to have a presence on the Internet and to do online marketing. As you will see in the following table, network marketing has great advantages over conventional marketing:

High entry cost
Low entry cost
Large entry barriers
No entry barriers
High mailing costs
No mailing costs
Delayed mail deliveries
Instantaneous mail delivery
Local, regional, national
International
From the office
From anywhere
During business hours
24 hours / 365 days
Punctual on-time ads
Permanent, ongoing ads
High cash investment
Little or no cash investment

Jay Abraham, a marketing expert, established three strategies to make your personal business a success:

1. Increase the number of clients.
2. Increase the volume of purchases.
3. Increase the frequency of purchases.

More clients, more purchases, and more often. Will you remember this? It's the "law of increases": *the more clients who buy, the more you'll have and with frequency.* How does one achieve it?

- To have more clients: ask for references.
- To increase the volume of purchases: cross-sell products and services.
- To increase the frequency: communicate regularly.

Simple, isn't it? Yes. Easy? No.

Easier said than done, I know. But does it really matter?

I suggest "low-cost marketing." I know of various strategies to make your potential customers know you. When you finish reading this section, you will have more selling tools. The proven techniques that follow have given me very good results.

Please take note of them:

Blogs, weblogs, newsletters. These are three of many ways to communicate with your audience. The easiest, quickest and most economical way is to start a theme blog. A website is your base camp in the network, and your newsletter is your digital newscast. You should put all these resources to work for your personal business.

Opinion articles. Build your image as an expert. The easy way is to express your opinion through various communications means. Perhaps the most affordable are the infinite number of publications that are online and offline. Always put your name with the link to your website.

Brochures and cards. Be professional in your brochures and business cards. Nothing is worse than a bad impression obtained from second class promotional material. Do you know what your potential client will think? "If I believe in his project, I will invest in it." Wear an impeccable image, it's half of your personal business. Another thing: it never ceases to amaze me when I meet people who are supposed to be in business but don't have a business card. How can they afford to lose an opportunity to market themselves?

Conferences. In business, it is essential to develop the ability to target your audiences by offering them lectures, conferences, seminars, debates ... Going out to sell is non-negotiable and you're the only one who can communicate like a professional. If you can do this, they will listen to your sales offer. You never know who is listening to you in the room. Based on my experience, I assure you that a lot of opportunities arise from giving lectures.

Real testimonials. Your satisfied clients are your best sales force. When a client congratulates you, ask his permission to use his testimonial on your website, conference, blog, brochure or where you need it. People who don't know you will believe more in what your clients say about you, not what you say about yourself.

Video promotion. Communications get more visually appealing each time. The young prefer to see than read - it's more visual, more direct and more enjoyable. You will need to edit small videos running for a few minutes to promote your business. You can upload them on your website or in your blog, or send them with your e-mails, now called "videomails." You can also create your own space with your videos in YouTube or Vimeo.

Network Marketing. Never dine alone. Use this time to strengthen your relationships and call on your friends or clients who you haven't seen in a long time. Relationships are everything in a personal business.

Database. Your personal business's most important asset is your database (it contains the names and details of existing clients and potential clients). Grow it, protect it legally, and communicate with them periodically. Because it contains the names of your existing and potential clients, they deserve information that's useful to them. Take care of your database and it will take care of you. The heart of any business is the client database. I recommend that you create it immediately, that you comply with the requirements of privacy protection laws and take care of this valuable asset as your most important treasure.

Newsletter and database. Regular contact with clients in your database is of maximum importance. Each e-mail you send to your clients keeps you in their minds, a way of maintaining a link so they don't cool off. I'm of the opinion that to receive, one has to give. It's important to offer value in your communications with clients in your database. If they appreciate your *newsletters*, they will ask for them if you don't send them (it happens to me). This is a good sign, it tells you that you're doing well. But if you receive a lot of requests to lower the frequency of your newsletter, this means something's wrong.

Pay per click ad campaigns of search engines. I am not fond of advertising, but I'm all for this type of advertising. The most popular are Google Adwords and Yahoo Advertising which offer you the possibility to highlight your website (sponsored links) in the first pages of the search engines. In return, you pay a small fee, which you fix, for every click in your link. It's a very powerful tool that will provide you with visitor traffic, for a monthly budget that you fix yourself.

Create your own ads online in the world's most popular search engine: Google. When users search on Google using one of the keywords you have chosen with your subject, your ad will appear in the results page of the search. This way, you drive your interested public to your subject. Users can click on your ad to obtain more information. In this case, pay per click will charge you a pre-determined number for you.

Exchanging links between related pages. Exchanging *links* with other websites and *blogs* is an effective marketing method for two reasons: one, it increases visitor traffic to linked websites, and two, search engines like Google give priority to websites that have *links* to other pages having the same related theme. As you already know, your website appearing on the first pages of search engines is of extreme importance, so I would advise you to include interesting *links* in your website. It's a marketing tool that is completely free.

Inclusion in Google and others search engines. One thing is to have a URL on Internet and the other is that the most important search engines know of its existence and gets indexed in their registries. To put your website in their registries is important so that users of search engines can find your web page. To do this, you must go to Google and register your URL - it's free. You can manage this on your own or ask your web master to do it for you (usually charged as an additional service when he takes care of your website). Never underestimate the power of the search engines to drive visitors to your website.

I use all the strategies described above, and some others that are beyond the scope of this work. I assure you that they work.

Afterword

Your financial situation is not going to change just reading this book. If you study the contents well, your mind will wake up and you begin to see opportunities where before you did not see any. Re-read the book and study it. Take action and apply the Money Code to your financial situation.

Let's do one more thing before wrapping up: give a copy to people in your life who can significantly benefit from it. With friends and family, form a study group for the book.

Get together with a group of people that you'd like to share the studying and reading of this book with. It is easier to achieve progress working in a team rather than on your own. If two minds multiply what can be achieved separately, imagine a focused group improving their relationships with money - it works like a laser beam. Get people to join so you can exchange different points of views and discuss the information provided in the book, it will be useful to everyone.

Although they are informal meetings, everyone must be encouraged to participate. I suggest that the duration of the meetings be one to two hours. The following options can be taken:

1. Everyone reads the book from the beginning to the end, or…
2. Each person takes a section.

At the end of the session, fix a date for the next appointment. Participants in the study group will read the text and prepare notes to raise the points they wish to comment on. In the group discussions, it is a good idea to provide personal examples to illustrate how the concepts in the book can be applied to inspire others to apply them as well.

The meetings can take place regularly. They can be done in the home of any one of the participants - or do it on rotation basis - or even in a cafeteria that is quiet.

If you decide to form a study group on this book, here are some guidelines that will help you:

1. In the first meeting, the group's common goal must be established.

2. It is advisable to have a moderator in each meeting. It doesn't have to be the same person each time. It would be useful to determine participation guidelines.

3. "Tasks" can be assigned which will consist of applying what was learned during the reading, and participants can comment on the results in the next meeting.

4. Book study groups don't need to have a start or finish date. It's not a course where you receive a diploma; but a process of learning that never ends.

Before I conclude this book, allow me to tell you a story. I have heard the following African story told at various times, and I believe that it is valid there as it is in our continent:

"Every morning in Africa, a gazelle wakes up. He knows that he has to run faster than the fastest lion if he doesn't want to die and be eaten up. Every morning in Africa, a lion wakes up. He knows that he has to run faster than the

slowest gazelle if he doesn't want to die of hunger. It doesn't matter if you're the lion or the gazelle. Each morning, when the sun rises, you begin to run all you can."

You've heard it: So whether you're an employee, a self-employed person, an entrepreneur - that is, whether you're a blue collar, white collar or gold collar - when the sun rises, better start running. Run, run, run!

About the Author

Follow him on social media.
Author's websites:

www.elcodigodeldinero.com
www.raimonsamso.com
www.institutodeexpertos.com
www.supermarketing.es
www.tiendasamso.com
http://raimonsamso.info

instagram.com/raimonsamso
youtube.com/raimonsamso
amazon.com/author/raimonsamso

EDICIONES INSTITUTO EXPERTOS

THE POWER OF DISCIPLINE

RAIMON SAMSÓ

THE HABIT THAT WILL CHANGE YOUR LIFE

THE MANIFESTATION CODE

12 Powers To Make Your Wishes Come True

EDICIONES INSTITUTO EXPERTOS

RAIMON **SAMSÓ**

COACHING FOR DAILY MIRACLES

GET MORE CLIENTS

HELP PEOPLE

SET THE STANDARD

RAIMON SAMSÓ

Note

I WOULD LIKE to ask you a favor, so that this book reaches more people, and that is for you to rate it with your honest review in the platform where you have bought it.

I will delegate the marketing of the book on the readers, because from this very point on I am already anxious to start writing a new book for you.

Blessings.

No part of this book may be reproduced, in any form or by any electronic means, without the express written authorization of the author, except for use in quotes, mentioning the source.

This book is licensed exclusively for personal use; it cannot be resold nor gifted to other people. If you want to share this book with someone else, please buy an additional license, acquiring a new digital copy. Thank you for respecting the author's work. That is the only way in which we can all avoid piracy, and in which the author will be able to publish more eBooks in the future.

All rights reserved, including the right to reproduce this book, or any part of it, in any form and format.

No fragment of this text may be reproduced, transmitted nor digitalized without the author's express authorization. The distribution of this book over the Internet or in any other form, without the express authorization of the author, is illegal and punishable by law.

The price of this book is especially low, so that any pocket can have access to it. Do not partake in digital piracy of protected material, it creates bad karma.